CourseBook Series

The CourseBook Series is the product of Dr. Mark H. Kavanaugh. Dr. Kavanaugh is a Professor of Psychology and Social Sciences at Kennebec Valley Community College. The CourseBooks contain the teaching content for each course.

Format

While definitively designed for digital distribution, each CourseBook is available in a number of formats. Distribution of the multi-touch ebook version is done exclusively through Apple Books. These CourseBooks may be purchased and downloaded directly to any iOS or Mac device.

Print versions of the CourseBooks are also available and are distributed through Amazon Kindle Unlimited.

Editing and Errors

Dr. Kavanaugh has written and edited all of this material but he is a horrible editor. He also cannot afford to have the work professionally reviewed. Mistakes, misspellings, broken links, and other errors may exist. Readers are encouraged to contact Dr. Kavanaugh directly to inform him of these errors for the next edition!

Copyright and Use

Dr. Kavanaugh owns the rights to the entire CourseBook. Others are free to use the CourseBook without permission. Graphics within the CourseBook are the original creations of Dr. Kavanaugh, downloaded from his Adobe Stock account, or are accompanied by attribution.

Index

How this CourseBook Works

The content of this CourseBook aligns with activities, expectations, and assignments that are found in the KVCC Learning Management System (LMS).

Students are expected to read and absorb the information in the CourseBook, read and review any textbook or other reading assignments, review the Assessment expectations outlined in each CourseBook Chapter, and participate in the expectations set by the instructor of the course in the LMS.

Chapter Organization

Each Chapter has been organized using an instructional design model called ALOTA, provides an outline of course materials that adheres to long-standing instructional design theory for adult learners. Namely, the model is greatly influenced by Gagne's Nine Events of Instruction

ALOTA

ALOTA is an acronym for the four essential parts of a lesson plan (or, in this case, chapter):

Attention
Learning Outcomes
Teaching
Assessment

Each Chapter in the CourseBooks series is organized in this manner in order to guide students through the material they are expected to learn.

Attention

Images, videos, text, and/or activities that bring readers into the focus of the lesson.

Learning Outcomes

Adhering to the language of Blooms Taxonomy of Learning Objectives, this section outlines the performance-based learning outcomes for the lesson. These align with the Assessment section of each lesson.

Teaching

This section can contain any variety of resources including text, lectures, recordings, videos, and links that provide a pathway through material to assist students in readying themselves for the Assessments.

Assessments

This section outlines assignments for students to demonstrate learning.

Additional Resources

QR Codes

In order to ensure that readers of the print version of this CourseBook can still access online content, I have included QR Codes (such as the one listed here under my icon for Dr. K's Psychobabble.)

Most smart phones are able to scan these codes with their camera and access the online material!

Apps in the CourseBook

Occasionally I will find mobile applications that relate to course content or are simply fun and engaging ways to learn. I will include links to these apps as the appear in the Apple App Store. It is likely that the same app is also available in Google Play but I will not usually provide the direct link to Google Play in the CourseBook.

Appendix

In the last section of each CourseBook you will find additional resources and information related to this course. Accessing Microsoft 365, a link to my YouTube Channel *Dr. K's Psychobabble,* and and introduction to APA Style are included in all of them, but some courses have additional appendix items.

Outcomes Alignment

Courses are designed to teach you a specific set of information and/or skills. These are largely determined by the specific learning outcomes through a course syllabus, in specific assignments and expectations, and in the structure of grading rubrics.

A course, however, often sits within a program that has learning outcomes associated with the expectations of external agents such as licensing board, accreditation, and other agencies.

This course rests in the Social Science / Psychology Department at Kennebec Valley Community College. The learning that is provided in this course is aligned with both the expectations of the American Psychological Associations guidelines for undergraduate Psychology education and with the Association of American Colleges and University's (AAC&U) VALUE structure.

This section provides you with information on how the learning activities (assignments, discussions, quizzes, etc.) align with the learning outcomes as designated by these external organizations.

Alignment With the Guidelines From the American Psychological Association

The American Psychological Association (APA) produces guidelines for the development of curriculum in the teaching of Psychology at the undergraduate level.

Here is a direct link to the document

The CourseBook series is designed to outline instructional materials and activities that demonstrate competence and knowledge in Psychology in alignment with these guidelines.

This section of each Psychology CourseBook will outline the specific content and activities (assessments) that align with the APA expectations.

Knowledge Base in Psychology

Describe key concepts, principles, and over arching themes in psychology.

- Chapter 1 Discussion - Clocks
- Chapter 1 Quiz - The DP
- Chapter 3 Discussion - Erikson's First Two Stages
- Chapter 4 Assignment - Erikson's First Three Stages in the Biography
- Chapter 5 Quiz - Concrete Operational Thinking
- Chapter 5 Quiz - Gardiner's Theory of Intelligences
- Chapter 6 Assignment - Marcia's Theory of Identity Status
- Chapter 7 Discussion A - Big 5 Personality Test
- Chapter 8 Discussion - Reflection on Flow
- Chapter 9 Quiz - Memory

Develop a working knowledge of psychology's content domains.

- Chapter 1 Discussion - Clocks
- Chapter 1 Quiz - The DP
- Chapter 3 Quiz - Myelination
- Chapter 3 Quiz - Assimilation and Accommodation

Describe applications of Psychology.

- Chapter 2 Discussion A - Traits
- Chapter 2 Quiz - Critical Periods

- Chapter 4 Quiz - Applications of Theory of Mind

- Chapter 5 Quiz - Gardener's Theory of Intelligence

- Chapter 5 Discussion A - Industry vs Inferiority

- Chapter 5 Discussion B - COVID and Industry

- Chapter 6 Discussion B - Adolescent Egocentrism

- Chapter 6 Quiz - Pre Frontal Cortex and Perspective Taking

- Chapter 6 Assignment - Marcia's Theory of Identity Status

- Chapter 9 Quiz - Memory in Late Life

- Interview Reflection Special Assignment

Scientific Inquiry and Critical Thinking

Use scientific reasoning to interpret psychological phenomena.

- Chapter 2 Discussion A - Traits

- Chapter 9 Quiz - Memory in Late Life

Demonstrate psychology Information Literacy.

- Biography Reflection Special Assignment

Engage in innovative and integrative thinking and problem solving.

- Chapter 7 Discussion B - Analysis of Puzzle Pieces

- Chapter 9 Discussion - Reflection on Aging

- Chapter 10 Assignment - Experiences of Loss

Interpret, design, and conduct basic psychological research.

- Chapter 7 Discussion A - Big 5 Personality Test

- Biography Special Assignment

Incorporate sociocultural factors in scientific inquiry.

- Chapter 2 Discussion B - Birthing

- Chapter 4 Discussion - Gender Identity

- Chapter 5 Quiz - Gardiner's Multiple Intelligences

- Chapter 10 Discussion - Experiences with Death

- Cultural Dimensions of Childbirth Special Assignment

- Interview Reflection Special Assignment

Ethical and Social Responsibility in a Diverse World

Apply ethical standards to evaluate psychological science and practice.

- Chapter 5 Discussion A - Industry vs Inferiority

- Chapter 6 Discussion A - Brain Development and Juvenile Justice

Build and enhance interpersonal relationships.

- Chapter 4 Assignment - Erikson's First Three Stages in the Biography

- Chapter 8 Quiz - Biography and Midlife

- Chapter 9 Quiz - Memory in Late Life

- Chapter 10 Assignment - Experiences of Loss

- Biography Special Assignment

Adopt values that build community at local, national, and global levels.

- Cultural Dimensions of Childbirth Special Assignment

Communication

Demonstrate effective writing for different purposes.

- Cultural Dimensions of Childbirth

- Biography Special Assignment

- Biography Reflection Special Assignment

Exhibit effective presentation skills for different purposes.

- Cultural Dimensions of Childbirth Special Assignment

Interact effectively with others.

- Chapter 4 Assignment - Erikson's First Three Stages in the Biography

- Chapter 8 Quiz - Biography and Midlife

- Biography Special Assignment

Professional Development

Apply psychological content and skills to career goals.

- Chapter 6 Assignment - Marcia's Theory of Identity Status

- Chapter 7 Quiz - Application of the Holland Test

- Identity Status Special Assignment

Exhibit self-efficacy and self-regulation.

- Chapter 2 Discussion A - Traits

- Chapter 10 Assignment - Analysis of an Obituary

Refine project management skills.

- Biography Special Assignment

Enhance teamwork capacity.

- Biography Special Assignment

Develop meaningful professional direction for life after graduation.

- Chapter 7 Quiz - Application of the Holland Test

- Identity Status Special Assignment

Alignment with the AAC&U VALUE Rubrics

In addition to the Learning Outcomes associated with the APA, specific to the field of Psychology, the Department has adopted additional learning outcomes as pretend in the structure of the VALUE Rubrics produced by the Association of American Colleges & Universities (AAC&U).

VALUE stands for "Value Added Learning for Undergraduate Education" and represents a national standard for the learning that should occur in undergraduate programs.

Below is a list of the specific expectations in this course that align with these outcomes.

Civic Engagement

- N/A

Creative Thinking

- Cultural Dimensions of Childbirth Special Assignment

- Biography Special Assignment

Critical Thinking

- Chapter 1 Quiz - The DP

- Chapter 2 Discussion A - Traits

- Chapter 4 Discussion - Non-Binary Gender Identity

- Chapter 5 Discussion A - Industry vs Inferiority

- Chapter 5 Discussion B - COVID and Industry

- Chapter 6 Assignment - Marcia's Theory of Identity Status

Ethical Reasoning

- Chapter 2 Discussion B - Birthing

- Chapter 4 Discussion - Non-Binary Gender Identity

- Chapter 5 Discussion A - Industry vs Inferiority

- Chapter 5 Discussion B - COVID and Industry

- Chapter 7 Assignment - Adult Job Description

- Chapter 10 Discussion - Experiences with Death

- Cultural Dimensions of Childbirth Special Assignment

Global Learning

- Cultural Dimensions of Childbirth Special Assignment

Information Literacy

- N/A

Inquiry and Analysis

- Chapter 5 Quiz - Gardiner's Multiple Intelligences

- Chapter 5 Discussion A - Industry vs Inferiority

- Chapter 5 Discussion B - COVID and Industry

- Chapter 6 Assignment - Marcia's Theory of Identity Status

- Chapter 7 Quiz - Application of the Holland Test

- Chapter 8 Discussion - Reflection on Flow

- Cultural Dimensions of Pregnancy Special Assignment

- Interview Reflection Special Assignment

Integrative Learning

- Chapter 5 Quiz - Gardiner's Multiple Intelligences

- Identity Status Special Assignment

- Interview Reflection Special Assignment

Intercultural Knowledge

- Cultural Dimensions of Childbirth Special Assignment

Lifelong Learning

- Biography Reflection Special Assignment

Oral Communication

- N/A

Problem Solving

- Chapter 4 Quiz - Applications of Theory of Mind

- Cultural Dimensions of Childbirth Special Assignment

Quantitative Literacy

- N/A

Reading

- N/A

Teamwork

- N/A

Written Communication

- Chapter 4 Assignment - Erikson's First Three Stages in the Biography

- Chapter 6 Assignment - Marcia's Theory of Identity Status

- Chapter 7 Assignment - Adult Job Description

- Chapter 10 Assignment - Experiences of Loss

- Cultural Dimensions of Childbirth Special Assignment

- Identity Status Special Assignment

- Biography Special Assignment

- Interview Reflection Special Assignment

Interpersonal Communication

- Chapter 4 Assignment - Erikson's First Three Stages in the Biography

- Chapter 8 Quiz - Biography and Midlife

- Chapter 9 Quiz - Memory in Late Life

- Chapter 10 Assignment - Experiences of Loss

- Biography Special Assignment

Developmental Psychology

This course is a survey of the biological, cognitive and socio-emotional aspects of human growth and development across the lifespan. Lifespan topics include an introduction to the lifespan perspective; biological changes; family, peer, and social relations; cognition; and personality development.

This CourseBook is designed to be used with a companion textbook.

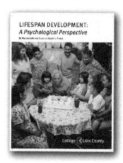

Lally, M. & Valentine-French, S.(2017). *Lifespan Development: A Psychological Perspective*. **Open Textbook Library**

This textbook can be accessed for **free**. It is available in **PDF** format.

Lifespan Development: A Psychological Perspective

Developmental Psychology, also known as Human Development or Lifespan Development, is the scientific study of ways in which people change, as well as stay the same, from conception to death. You will no doubt discover in the course of studying that the field examines change across a broad range of topics. These include physical and other psychophysiological processes, cognition, language, and psychosocial development, including the impact of family and peers.

Changes made to this Edition of the CourseBook

1. Standard sizing of text.

2. Chapter 1 - Revised all the material on the Historical Clock and Generations.

3. Chapter 2 - Changed Attention section from the work of Francis Galton to current work on the fetus and music.

4. Chapter 3 - Added link to the Attachment Project.

5. Chapter 3 - Added a question about attachment to Chapter 3 Discussion.

6. Chapter 5 - Added information on Anti-dopamine parenting.

7. Chapter 5 - Added material on Cattell's theory of intelligence (fluid and crystalized intelligence).

8. Chapter 6 - Discussion A changed to focus on the development of Formal Operational thinking.

9. Chapter 7 - Took out Emerging Adulthood resources that were broken.

10. Chapter 7 - Added movie on when adulthood begins.

11. Chapter 7 - Added paragraph in Puzzle Pieces pertaining to negative parental role models and the ability we have to choose to NOT imitate them.

12. Chapter 9 - Added additional information on Fluid and Crystalized Intelligence.

13. Chapter 9 - Added material on personalty changes after 60.

14. Chapter 9 - Added video on Successful Aging.

15. Added Appendix items including "Microsoft 365", "Monitor on Psychology", and "Dr. K's Psychobabble".

16. General edits and clean up.

About the Author

Mark H. Kavanaugh, Ph.D.

Mark Kavanaugh has been writing, teaching, and integrating technology into instruction for decades. He holds a Masters in Counseling, Masters in Instructional and Performance Technology, and a Ph.D. in Educational Psychology. Mark lives in Maine with his wife Katie.

Visit Mark's Website

Introduction to Lifespan Development

1

Attention

In the Movies

This course tackles the challenging subject of change. How we change over time. The themes of this course have been capturing our imaginations and have appeared in poems, stories, songs, books, and movies.

To prepare this section I looked up the following categories of movies. The number in each category was astounding. What might make these movies great is that we relate to the characters in them. They are us. They are where we once were, or they are where we are going to be someday.

Movies about Parenting

- Parenthood
- Raising Arizona
- Three Men and a Baby

Movies about Childhood

- Inside Out

- A Christmas Story
- It
- Harry Potter

Movies about Growing Up

- Dead Poets Society
- Juno
- The Breakfast Club

Movies about Marriage

- Emma
- Little Women
- Daddy's Home

Movies about Midlife

- Crazy, Stupid, Love
- Thelma and Louise
- The Bridges of Madison County

Movies about Aging

- Harold and Maude
- Driving Miss Daisy
- Grumpy Old Men

Movies about Dying

- The Bucket List
- On Golden Pond
- Tuesdays with Morrie

Learning Outcomes

Upon completion of this Chapter, students should be able to:

1. Discuss examples of the Developmental Clocks.

2. Apply the Developmental Perspective to a psychological question.

3. Plan a Case Study Interview research study on a single individual.

Teaching

Note on Teaching: This section will describe all the material that you ned to review to complete the Assessment section successfully. While this section is akin to a "Lecture" in class, not all the information you need to complete the assessments are contained in these pages. Other sources such as your textbook, Online resources, movies, etc. may need to be reviewed.

Do People Change?

Have you every wondered if someone was every going to change? Have you ever tried to make that happen? If so, you know how hard that can be! But I have a surprise for you. People change all the time! They don't always change in the ways we would like them to change, but, they do change.

Studying Psychology

The prerequisite for this course is Introduction to Psychology. In that course you learned about the brain, consciousness, sensation and perception, learning, thinking, memory, emotion, and personality. Each of these things was learned as a part of the human experience and we learned what they were and how they manifest in our lives.

Each of these characteristics that we studied in Introduction to Psychology, however, are not the same throughout lifespan. They change. Our brain changes from the time we are born until we die, our memory capacity changes as we age, even our emotions and our ability to manage them changes over time (thank heavens!)

Why we Study Developmental Psychology

Let me create a scenario. You are a nurse and you are have a patient who has just been diagnosed with Type II Insulin Dependent Diabetes. They have to learn how to check their blood sugar levels, eat properly, and how to inject themselves with insulin when they need it.

How are you going to plan to do this?

One of the first questions you are going to ask is "How old is the patient?" (Or at least this **should** be one of the first questions you are going to ask!

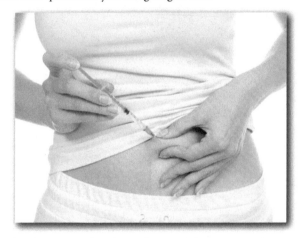

Why do you need to know how old the patient is?

Based on how old the patient is, you are going to **modify** how you approach the teaching. If the patient is really young, you may decide to use a teddy bear to explain the process. If the patient is older and married you may elicit the help of family members.

These are just some of the ways that you are going to modify what you do with the patient based on their age...so how do you know what modifications to make? You study Developmental Psychology!

Normative Development

This book, as you will see, focuses on **normative development**, the patterns and trends that are common to the most people. But, what really is normal? We know that within the concept of **normal** is a LOT of diversity. Two people can be very different and both can still be considered "normal." Here is how the field of Psychology approaches the concept of normal.

Since "normal" is common, we can understand what is normal by understanding what is "abnormal."

We define abnormal based on three criteria:

1. **Statistics** - abnormal behavior is rare. Less than 2% of the population.

2. **Social Norms** - abnormal behavior violates the expectations of someone's culture.

3. **Dysfunction** - abnormal behavior interferes with the individuals functioning in their role in society.

Pretty much all three of these may need to be met for a behavior to be considered "abnormal" This does not mean that behaviors that don't meet these criteria are not, at times problematic, but they would not meet this strict criteria.

The Developmental Perspective

Through this course you are going to be learning how to take the "Developmental Perspective" or DP.

The DP is very simple. When we are faced with a question in Psychology we affirm that the answer to that question may very well be impacted by how OLD the person is.

In this class we will be studying what NORMALLY happens across the lifespan and based on that knowledge we can take the DP on any topic. Here are some examples:

"How does divorce effect the children?"

This is obviously a great question, but for this class it is incomplete. Before we can really answer this question we need to know how old the kids are. We know that changes in family structure can have profound impacts on an individual but these impacts will be different based on how old the person is.

Let's say the person we are asking this about is 10 years old. What is "normally" going on in the life of a 10-year old that may be impacted by a divorce?

What if the person we are asking this about is 17? What if they are 25? What if they are 50? (Remember, a di-

vorce can happen at any time in the lifespan). It should be apparent to you now that it is quite difficult to answer a question without asking how old the person is.

Note: Taking the DP is not the same as applying Developmental Theory. You are NOT taking the DP when you ask something like "How does intelligence change over childhood?" or if you ask "How does memory change in late adulthood?" These are simply applications of theory and knowledge.

The DP **adds age** to the equation of a question that is not about age. So we ask questions like these:

1. How well do people remember things?
2. How fast can a person learn a new skill?
3. How will losing a job impact a person?
4. How will having children impact a person's plans?
5. How will a serious injury impact someone?

The answer to each of these questions is the same - It depends on how old the person is!

Developmental Perspective

So, to apply the DP to each of these questions, we would rewrite them as follows (and these are just examples, you can apply any age...)

1. How well does a 3 year old remember things?

2. How fast can a 12 year old learn a new skill?

3. How will losing a job impact a 55 year old?

4. How will having children impact a 13 year old's plans?

5. How will a serious injury impact 6 year old?

Normative Development

This course is going to focus on normative development. We are going to explore the ways in which people normally change over time. That way when you know how old a person is, you can simply look at your Developmental Psychology class and see where they should be in terms of memory, emotions, social interac-

Sometimes
I pretend
to be NORMAL.
—
but it gets boring.
—
so i go back to being me.

tions, etc. etc. That way you can use this information to guide your practice.

We are going to be looking at the following areas of normative development:

1. Normative age-graded influences - changes that occur because of maturation, genetic influences, that are common among all people of a certain age.

2. Normative history-graded influences - changes due to the **cohort** you were born into. This is based on the year you were born. (We will go a bit more into this when we talk about the **Historical Clock**)

3. Non-normative life influences - these are the occurrences of things in our lives at specific ages and how it may impact our development.

The Field of Developmental Psychology

As we get ready to take this journey we need to remember that Developmental Psychology (or Lifespan Development) is a complex field.

1. Development is lifelong - changes happen throughout our lifespan (this was not always thought to be the case.)

2. Development is multidirectional - we experience changes in various areas of our life simultaneously across physical, cognitive, and psychosocial domains.

3. Development is multidisciplinary - this field takes into consideration the complementary sciences of Sociology, Anthropology, Human Biology, Genetics, and many other fields.

4. Development is characterized by **plasticity**. Plasticity refers to the change and adapt to different influences.

5. Development is multicontextual - development occurs in many contexts and is influence by culture, values, social circumstances, history, etc.

Some Apps to Consider

The following apps have been developed by the Northern Ireland Central Care Council. The apps are made for iPhone size screens (no iPad version is available) but they will still run on an iPad!

Since the apps are developed outside the US, availability may not always be secure. In addition, at least one of the apps needs to be updated to work with the new version of iOS. So, enjoy these as you can as an extra bonus to the course material.

Developmental Clocks

Your book refers to these as ages, whereas I am going to refer to them as the **Developmental Clocks**. When we consider that we are continually aging we can imagine a clock ticking away as time goes by in our lives.

The truth is, we have multiple clocks ticking at the same time. Each of these is marking time in different areas of our development and in different influences on our development.

Biological Clock

You are probably already familiar with this one! The biological clock represents the maturation of our bodies and minds through the genetic time table. The biological clock determines when we will learn to go potty, when we can have children, our first gray hair, and when we will die.

We might hear about the Biological Clock when we consider women who are thinking of having children. There is a time frame during which this is possible (and more safe.)

Psychological Clock

The Psychological Clock is the one that marks time in the development of our emotions, emotional control, cognitive abilities (thinking, memory, learning, etc.) and our maturity.

Already you might be noting that sometimes the Biological Clock and the Psychological Clock are not always in sync! We all know someone who is unusually mature and responsible "for their age" and we all know someone who is not as "mature" as they should be for their age!

Social Clock

The "should" mentioned above could also be seen as part of the Social Clock. The Social Clock marks out what you SHOULD be able to do or be doing at a particular age based on the social norms and values of a culture.

It may be that in your family it was expected that you would move out of the home, get a job (or go to school), and start your life right around the age of 18-21. If you were 35 years old and still living at home, still dependent on your parents, this would be seen as "wrong" and in violation of the expectations of your culture. This would be a violation of the Social Clock.

Historical Clock and the Generations

A very popular way of characterizing the different historical clocks is by the use of the concept of generations. There is a great website (linked on the previous page) that outlines the generations from the point of view of marketing.

The following is a submission by a former student named Lisa Blue. I believe it does a good job in describing the work-related experiences of differently aged individuals. However, this description is the perspective of ONE person. There is actually a lot of diversity within each group and no one should be offended if the description does not describe them. Here is her perspective:

Historical Clocks in the Workplace by Lisa Blue

The historical clock refers to characteristics that is associated with being raised in a specific time. This is typically categorized with generation names such as Baby-Boomers or Gen X.

One situation where it is very easy to see the distinctions between these generations is in the workplace.

I worked for years at the UMF Computer Center. Our director was what was considered in the Veterans group, the programmers were Baby Boomers, the networking and technicians, and myself were Generation X, and all of my student workers were Generation Y. It was very interesting to witness the different work ethics, management styles, and just ideas on life in general.

The "Great Generation"

For example, our "Veteran" director rarely checked his email, and preferred paper to digital. When he spoke, he took his time to answer a question, and responded with a "silver-tongue" as it were. He was extremely frugal when it came to the budget, and his management style was, while calm and listening, did expect solid efficient results. He worked over 80 hours a week, and rarely took any days off. Retirement was not even on his radar.

Baby Boomers

Our Baby-Boomers were very into the technology, communicated mostly with email, worked a normal 40-60 hours a week, and their management style was a little more lenient than the director. Many were looking

Five Generations Working Side by Side in 2020

TRADITIONALISTS	**BOOMERS**	**GEN X**	**MILLENNIAL**	**GEN 2020**
Born 1900-1945	Born 1946-1964	Born 1965-1976	Born 1977-1997	After 1997
Great Depression	Vietnam, Moon Landing	Fall of Berlin Wall	9/11 Attacks	Age 15 and Younger
World War II	Civil/Women's Rights	Gulf War	Community Service	Optimistic
Disciplined	Experimental	Independent	Immediacy	High Expectations
Workplace Loyalty	Innovators	Free Agents	Confident, Diversity	Apps
Move to the 'Burbs'	Hard Working	Internet, MTV, AIDS	Social Everything	Social Games
Vaccines	Personal Computer	Mobile Phone	Google, Facebook	Tablet Devices

Generations X, Y, Z, and the Others

forward to retirement, and had plans on how they were going to spend their time with travel.

Generation X

Now comes my Gen X. Technology is a huge part of our daily lives, and emails overtake the use of phone calls. Our cell phones are nearby at all times. Personally, I felt that I had a lot of opportunities and could work to accomplish anything I wanted. I certainly didn't mind starting from the bottom to work my way up in my career. I tried to think ahead towards retirement, so I saved my money as much as I could (still do). My work week was never less than 50 hours, and basically I was on call 24/7, as most IT positions are. My management style was fair, fun, focused on team work, yet not afraid to set boundaries and consequences.

Generation Y

My student workers had a very different work ethic. I would typically have to bribe several of them to show up to work on time. Constant texting and social media on the job was a constant problem. They didn't care much for authority, or feedback. And if they didn't like what we managers had to say, they could simply walk out because they could get another job in a heartbeat. Not to say that there weren't some excellent work-study students, but in general they fit the stereo-typical characteristics of the Gen Y category. They have many more options educationally and career-wise. They were raised in a society that "everyone wins", so receiving negative feedback or constructive criticism is not well-received. There is also a sort of sense of entitlement as well. On a priority scale, social time and fun ranked high, and work at the bottom.

The Historical Clock in the workplace isn't always so chronological. These days you find more Gen Xers or even Gen Y (or Nexters), in management positions over Baby Boomers. This can cause a disconnect in communication between managers and employees. Also there can be a decrease in morale in some workers whose managers are younger than the employee. Unfortunately, it probably won't be long until I'm in such a position.

Gen Z and Alpha

The newest generations are Gen Z (1997-2012) and Gen Alpha (2010-2025).

How are defining Gen Z and Gen Alpha, and why?

Generations Around the World

While the categories of people described above originate in American thought and literature, they are used widely around the globe. The events that led to these categories (such as WWII, the Great Depression, and technology changes) were global. Some countries came up with different names to describe these generations, such as Australia's name for the Greatest Generation is the "Federalist Generation."

Generations Around the Globe

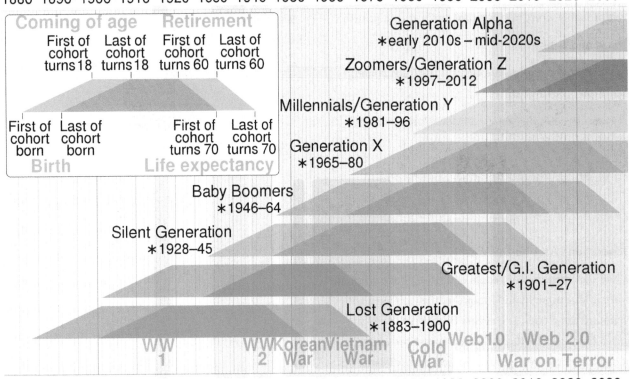

1880 1890 1900 1910 1920 1930 1940 1950 1960 1970 1980 1990 2000 2010 2020 2030

Coming of age   Retirement

First of   Last of   First of   Last of
cohort   cohort   cohort   cohort
turns 18   turns 18   turns 60   turns 60

First of   Last of   First of   Last of
cohort   cohort   cohort   cohort
born   born   turns 70   turns 70

Birth   Life expectancy

Generation Alpha
∗early 2010s – mid-2020s

Zoomers/Generation Z
∗1997–2012

Millennials/Generation Y
∗1981–96

Generation X
∗1965–80

Baby Boomers
∗1946–64

Silent Generation
∗1928–45

Greatest/G.I. Generation
∗1901–27

Lost Generation
∗1883–1900

WW
1

WW
2

Korean
War

Vietnam
War

Cold
War

Web 1.0   Web 2.0

War on Terror

1880 1890 1900 1910 1920 1930 1940 1950 1960 1970 1980 1990 2000 2010 2020 2030

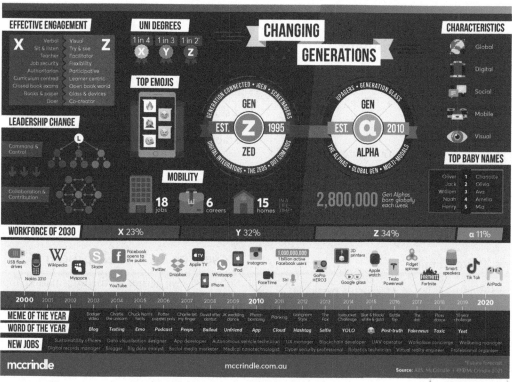

The image above is only part of a much larger infographic comparing Gen Z and Gen Alpha.

Access the full infographic here.

Major Themes in Development

There are a number of themes that are outlined within different theories of human development.

Nature vs. Nurture

This long held question examines the degree to which a trait or characteristic is more influenced by genetics or the environment that the person grows up in. As simple as this can seem, it is the focus of a lot on controversy, particularly in issues like intelligence.

Continuity vs. Discontinuity

This theme examines the degree to which a particular line of development happens through slow, imperceptible transitions or through distinct qualitative or quantitative stages. These will be apparent when we begin to look at our stage-based theories.

Active vs. Passive

This particular theme examines the degree to which we have influence over our own development, or does it just happen whether we are involved or not.

Stability vs. Change

This debate is particularly evident in the study of topics such as personality and intelligence. Do we have stable personalities over time? Is our intelligence the same no matter what our age is?

Research in Development

So how do we gather all the information about how people change? We conduct research! There are many ways in which we conduct research in development.

In order to gather the data needed to understand and interpret the patterns and theories that explain human development, a number of research methods are utilized.

Case Study

The case study is an intensive examination of the factors related to the development of a single individual. The results are usually very subjective, but they provide insight into the ways in which certain factors may impact development.

You know one case study very well...YOU! Your current understanding of how factors impact development is largely based upon a select number of case studies including yourself and people you know.

While this information is valuable it is limited to your subjective observations, memory, and reinterpretation based on other motivations.

The same applies to how much we generalize (assume that something is true for everyone) based on any one case study.

Observation

A closely aligned method for learning about how people develop is through systematic observation. The term "systematic" is important because we want to be able to observe others using a consistent method. We might, for instance, watch a group of teenagers hanging out at the mall or some children playing in the playgroups. It can be said that these types of observations are often what trigger individuals to study Psychology in the first place. We see something fascinating happen around us and we want to know more.

Many psychologists across history were able to cite the incident or observation they made that brought them into their lifelong obsession with studying Psychology!

Survey

One of the most widely used research methods is the survey. There are many ways in which a survey could be conducted including the following:

1. Asking questions to your subject and recording their responses on a form.

2. Having the subject fill out the form themselves.

3. Mailing the form to your subjects.

4. Completing the form Online.

Surveys are used a lot because they are very inexpensive to administer (just send it out in an email!) However, there are a lot of problems with surveys.

1. People could falsify their answers (either because they are not taking the survey seriously or they want to portray themselves in a better light.)

2. People may not understand the question or the type of answers they can provide.

3. Poorly designed survey questions may lead to specific kinds of answer patterns.

4. There may be significant and related (to your research study) differences between people who participate in surveys and those who do not.

Interviews

This method can be used to gather information through the use of a survey, open ended conversation, and structured questions. It can be conducted on ONE person (case study) or it can be part of a series of interviews across a broad number of people (interviewing a number of people impacted by the Government Shutdown of 2019) or it can be done in a group (focus groups.)

Psychophysiological Assessment

Researchers may record physiological data such as heart rate, respiration, or cortical steroid levels in your blood to determine the physiological aspects of the behavior they are observing.

They typical **polygraph** or the **lie detector** is an example of this. Users of the polygraph purport that they can tell when someone is lying based on the changes they experience in respiration, heart rate, blood pressure, and sweating.

Secondary Information

Another way in which we may explore topics in development is to examine existing records. These records can come from a number of sources including hospital records, Census data, State statistical data, etc. Some researchers even look at the data inside many other studies. This type of research is called a **meta analysis** and it tries to examine larger trends that may not be apparent in a single study, but manifest when we combine all those studies together.

Laboratory Observations or Experiments

Sometimes, when we want to learn more about a very specific aspect of development, we may design experiments in a lab setting that allow us to control as many of the factors as possible in order to isolate the importance of one particular factor.

Later in the course we will see some interesting and innovative experiments that were conducted by researchers into early childhood cognitive abilities. These contrived situations do not reflect how a person really expresses these skills in the real world but it does allow for a fair comparison among people because the experimental conditions are identical.

Correlation Studies

Correlation studies are those that collect data in order to determine if one factor has a relationship (causal or not) with another factor. This is likely the most common statistic that we hear in current studies. Many researchers will describe the results of their study in terms of **correlations** that occurred between variables.

Some example questions that we may ask include:

1. What is the relationship between family socioeconomic status and achievement in grade school?

2. What is the relationship between hours studying and GPA?

3. What is the relationship between the use of corporal punishment as a child and future domestic violence?

4. What is the relationship between time spent playing "violent video games" and actual violence in schools?

Each of these may elicit a response from you that implies a causal (cause and effect) relationship between these, but the correlation study only determines of the two factors are related, not that one caused the other.

There can be two types of correlation relationships (and varied strength of these relationships.)

1. **Positive Correlation** - this means that when one goes up the other goes up as well. When one goes down the other goes down. We might find that when we increase the amount of time we are studying our GPA goes up as well. When we decrease our study time, our grades go down.

2. **Negative Correlation** - negative, in this context, does not mean "bad." It simply means that as one factor goes up the other goes down. An example of this might be the amount of television we watch and the amount of homework we get done. A study may indicate that the more we watch TV the less homework we do, the less we watch TV the more homework we do.

Here is a great web resource on correlations, causal effects, and the Pearson Product Moment Correlation Coefficient!

Correlation on Simple Psychology

Research over Time

One of the challenges for conducting studies in human development is that we need to be able to capture how things change over time. The challenge is that the researcher is aging as well! If we are going to examine how things change over time we can use ALL of the above mentioned methods in a developmental way.

Longitudinal Study

The most challenging of these is the longitudinal study. This approach applies research methods to an individual or group of individuals over a span of time. If we are looking at factors that change over the life of a person, we are going to need a structure in the study that will allow multiple generations of researchers to work together, and sadly, the originator of the study may not live to see the results!

Good Genes are Nice, but Joy is Better

In 1938, the Harvard Study of Adult Development set out to follow 268 Harvard Sophomores through their lives. The study has been ongoing for 80 plus years. The study has changed over time to include other groups of people, but it still represents one of the largest longitudinal studies about aging ever conducted.

Explore the Harvard Second Generation Study looking at the offspring of the 1st Generation!

Cross Sectional Study

Another method, and popular because researchers get to see their results, is the cross sectional method. This method conducts research across a number of **age cohorts**. Age cohorts are groups of people who are the same age. We might, for example, want to study memory across the lifespan. We design a study that measures memory among a group of 5-year-olds, 12-year-olds, 20-year-olds, 35-year-olds, and 55-year-olds.

Differences between these groups can be attributed to changes in their development over time!

Sequential Research

This is simply a combination of both methods, longitudinal and cross-sectional.

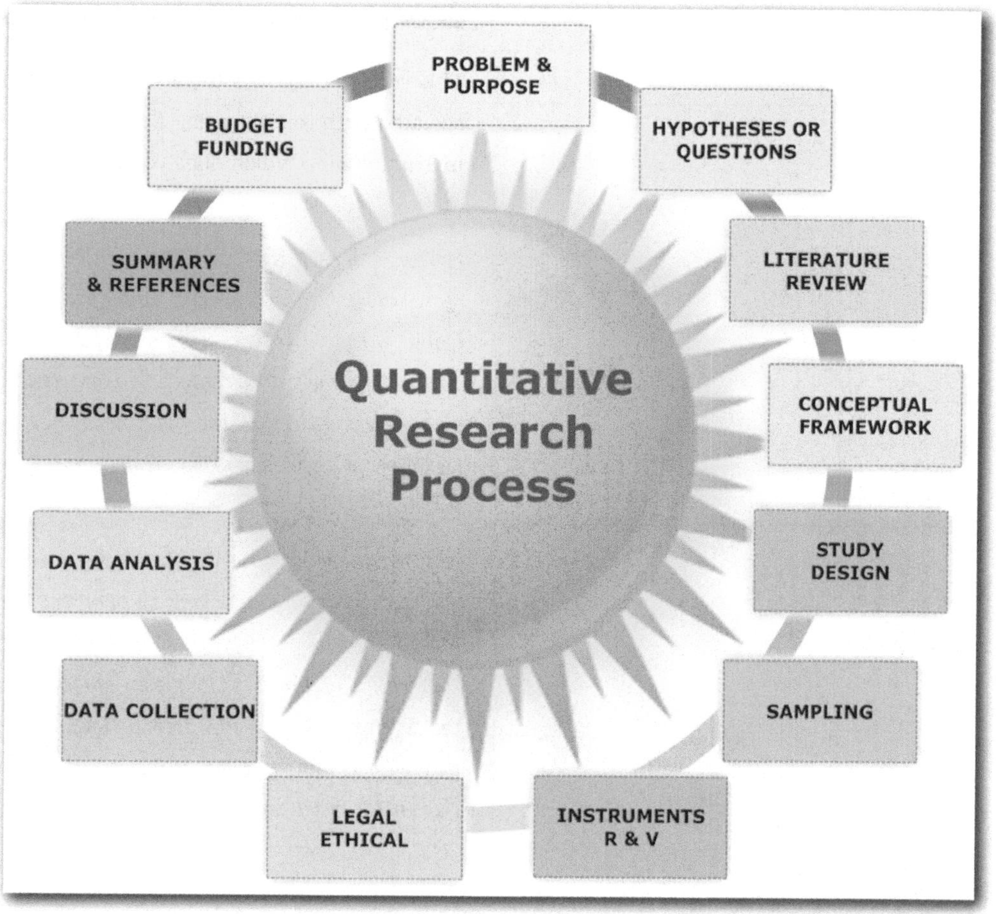

Quantitative Research Process

- PROBLEM & PURPOSE
- HYPOTHESES OR QUESTIONS
- LITERATURE REVIEW
- CONCEPTUAL FRAMEWORK
- STUDY DESIGN
- SAMPLING
- INSTRUMENTS R & V
- LEGAL ETHICAL
- DATA COLLECTION
- DATA ANALYSIS
- DISCUSSION
- SUMMARY & REFERENCES
- BUDGET FUNDING

Assessment

This section describes the activities and assignments associated with this Chapter. Be sure to check with your instructor as to which ones you are expected to complete.

Note regarding Discussions: These activities are primarily geared toward students who are taking the course in either an Online or Hybrid format. It is expected that students will post an answer to the prompt contained in the section below and reply to at least two other students' posts in order to obtain full credit for the discussion. All posts must be substantive and contribute to the discussion.

Note regarding Assignments: These activities entail the creation of a "document" of sorts that needs to be sent to your instructor. Most of these may be papers. All papers must be submitted to the identified "Drop Box" for the assignment and must be in either Microsoft Word or PDF format. Pay attention to expectations such as title pages and APA formatting if these are indicated in the instructions.

Other assignments may entail different types of "documents" including presentations, artwork, charts, spreadsheets, and/or movies. Instructions on how to submit these will be included in the descriptions below

Though they will not be repeated, all of the above notes should be assumed in subsequent chapters, unless otherwise indicated.

Chapter 1 Discussion - Clocks

In this discussion I want you to provide an example of ONE clock and how it manifests in your life. You can tell a story or simply state a fact about yourself. Here are some examples:

1. I was born during the "Cold War" when the threat of Nuclear War was very present and on our minds. This is part of my Historical Clock and impacts the way I view the world.

2. I had my first child when I was in my early 30's. This makes me an older father than some other fathers. This could be an example of Biological or Social clock...according to the social clock I "should" have had kids by then!

Just post ONE example of ONE clock. Respond to each other's postings as appropriate.

Chapter 1 Quiz - The DP

1. Write a typical psychological question.

2. Write that same question again but apply an example of the Developmental Perspective.

Planning a Case Study Interview

An essential aspect of this course is the Biography Interview and Reflection. These assignments our outlined in the Special Assignments chapter in this CourseBook.

Heredity, Prenatal Development and Birth

2

Attention

A Fetus and Music

When we think of the environment that a fetus lives in we need to understand that they are quite aware of what is going on around them. We have known, for instance, that children recognize their mother's voice very soon after birth.

This article focuses on how the fetus responds to music and other sounds.

A Fetus and Music

Learning Outcomes

Upon completion of this Chapter, students should be able to:

1. Identify the potential impact of the introduction of a teratogen during critical periods of development.

2. Describe what is meant by cephalocaudal and proximodistal development.

3. Discuss the source of personal traits and how they fit into the models of Genetic Environmental Correlations.

4. Discuss the pros and cons related to home child birth and other alternative birthing methods.

Teaching

Nature vs. Nurture

Is it nature or is it nurture? This is one of the most significant questions we ask in the study of Human Development. The answer is always the same...it is BOTH! But we want to know to what degree is a particular trait inherited versus the degree to which the particular trait is learned through experience.

Some Basic Genetics

If you have not taking a Biology class then here is a little bit on genetics. Each of the cells in our body (with the exception of our reproductive cells, eggs and sperm) have the same set of genetic material as all the other cells in the body. Half of that genetic material we inherited from our mothers, the other half from our fathers.

23
pairs of chromosomes
(with some exceptions)

MOVIE - Learn how genes work!

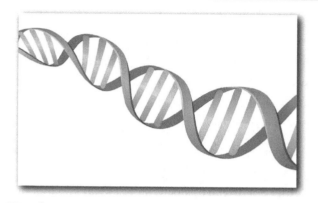

We refer our endowment of genetic material as our **genes**. Our genes are organized into structures within our cells called **chromosomes** of which we have 23 pairs. 22 of these pairs are fairly identical in length, the 23rd pair is our sex chromosomes (the ones that determine our sex and carry sex-related genetic codes), can be different in length. An XY configuration of the sex chromosome means that the person's sex is male, an XX configuration of the sex chromosome means that the person's sex is female.

Not all of the genetic material we have in each cell is "expressed" or "activated." The genes that determine a function of a cell (a nerve cell vs. a muscle cell) will be activated to determine the function of that cell. In addition, we may have aspects of our genetic material that are simply not expressed because they are dominated by stronger genetic material. So some genes are said to be **dominant** (and will express), while others are said to be **recessive** (and those will not express.)

The totality of our genetic endowment is called our **genotype**. The expressed part of our genetic endowment is called our **phenotype**.

Problems with Genes

Sometimes there can be a problem with the way the genetic code is copied from generation to generation. Problems that occur at the genetic level are called **Genetic Disorders**. There are some genetic disorders that are coded in dominant genes, others are more rare because they are coded in recessive genes.

On p. 37 of your book there is an excellent table with quite a number of the known genetic disorders listed.

Child with Down's Syndrome

Sometimes the problem that occurs with genes is that there are missing or too many of a particular gene. These are referred to as **Chromosomal Disorders**.

One of the more famous of these is **Downs Syndrome**, or **Trisomy 21**. Individuals with Downs Syndrome have an extra 21st chromosome. Thy typically have intellectual disabilities and certain physical features such as short fingers and toes, folds of skin over the eyes, and a protruding tongue.

Another set of chromosome disorders are those that occur specific to the 23rd pair, or the sex chromosome. **Turner Syndrome** occurs when all or part of one of the X chromosomes is lost resulting in reduced cognitive functioning and sexual maturation. Another is **Klinefelter's Syndrome** where the 23rd chromosome is composed of an extra X chromosome (XXY). The Y chromosome stimulates the development of male genitalia, but the extra X chromosome inhibits maturation.

Genetic Counseling

Since some of the genetic disorders are not dominant, some couples seek out genetic counseling to determine

MOVIE - Learn more "I am a Genetic Counselor"

the likelihood of having a child with a specific condition.

Behavioral Genetics

The questions of Nature vs. Nurture are really explored in the field of Behavioral Genetics. Essentially, Behavioral Genetics examines the interplay between genetics and the environment on behavior. It is important to recognize that the relationship between genetics and the environment is **reciprocal**. This means that the environment can impact the expressions of genes, but genes can also impact the environment. Consider these perspectives:

Genotype Environment Correlations - Process by which genetic factors contribute to variations in the environment.

1. **Passive Genotype Environment Correlations** - children passively inherit the genes and the environment of their parents. *Let's say that athletic ability and the opportunity for athletics occur in an athletic family.*

2. **Evocative Genotype Environment Correlations** - social environments react to individuals based upon their inherited characteristics. *The temperament of a child or the presence of a disorder will cause the environment to change.*

3. **Active Genotype Environment Correlations** - individuals seek out environments that support their genetic tendencies. *This can be seen if one individual is a musician or has a different sexual orientation...both may seek out specific environments that will support them.*

Genotype Environment Interactions - these involve genetic susceptibility to the environment. *Children who may have inherited a susceptibility to a mental health disorder, may display less problems if they are raised by parents who are very structured.*

Prenatal Development

The prenatal environment is, of course, the first environment we experience. In this section we will first outline the developmental stages of normal that occur in utero (while still in the uterus) and then explore **teratogens** (simply, any external event, condition, or substance that can impact the development of an unborn child.)

Germinal, Embryonic, and Fetal Periods

The gestation period of a person is divided into three distinct periods.

1. **Germinal** - about 14 days from fertilization - the germinal period lasts from the time of fertilization to the implantation of the fertilized egg into the wall of the placenta. This fertilized egg is called the **zygote** and cellular division and differentiation has already started to occur by the time the implantation happens.

2. **Embryonic** - starts in about the third week gestation - the implanted embryo continues to undergo cellular division and differentiation. The protective **placenta** develops to nourish the embryo. The cellular division and differentiation follows two pathways of development:

   1. **Cephalocaudal** - meaning head to tail, so development happens first in the head and then moves down the rest of the body.

   2. **Proximodistal** - means inner to outer, so development happens from the midline and them moves out to distal parts of the body.

3. **Fetal** - from about the 9th week gestation until birth - at this point the organism is recognized as a **fetus** and has all of its body parts in some stage of development.

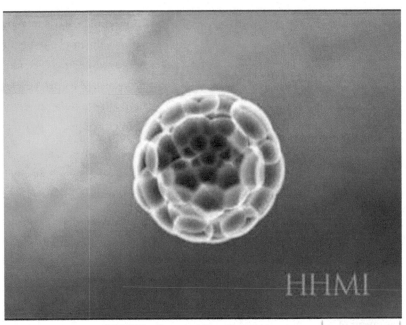

MOVIE - Prenatal Development

Prenatal Brain Development

As you can see from the image above regarding critical periods, the development of the nervous system is continuous throughout gestation. Brain development is a fascinating aspect of human development and some pretty amazing things happen!

Starting from a relatively undifferentiated set of stem cells, the brain forms as illustrated in this image.

As the individual cells become the brain, a number of processes are happening.

1. Neuron Proliferation

2. Neuron Differentiation

3. Neuron Migration

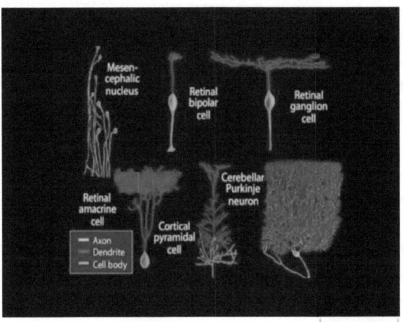

MOVIE - Neurogenesis

Brain Development During Gestation / At Birth

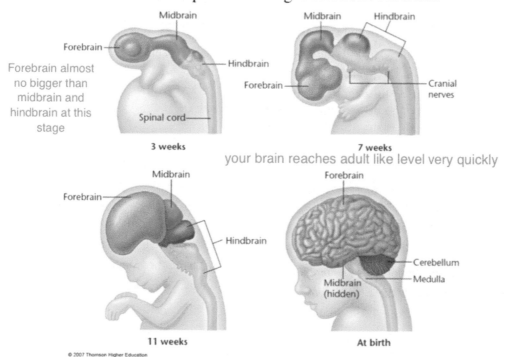

Forebrain almost no bigger than midbrain and hindbrain at this stage

Midbrain

Forebrain

Hindbrain

Spinal cord

3 weeks

Midbrain

Hindbrain

Forebrain

Cranial nerves

7 weeks

your brain reaches adult like level very quickly

Midbrain

Forebrain

Hindbrain

11 weeks

Forebrain

Cerebellum

Medulla

Midbrain (hidden)

At birth

At Birth = 350g, At 1 year = 1000g (adult = 1,200 to 1,400g)

Critical Periods and Teratogens

Development follows a strict timeline that prescribes periods of time where organs undergo genesis during a particular span of time. We call these stand a "critical period" because it is critical that nothing interfere with development during this time as it may adversely impact the development of that organ.

Teratogens is a term used to describe environmental factors that could lead to birth defects. Although we may have heard about some straight forward teratogens, such as smoking while pregnant and drinking alcohol, just about anything can be a potential teratogen.

Our textbook lists a good number of them and provides some details and examples of how these have been found to impact fetal development:

1. Alcohol

2. Tobacco

3. Prescription and over-the-counter medications

4. Illicit drugs

5. Pollutants

6. Toxoplasmosis

7. STDs

8. HIV

9. German Measles

Alcohol is listed first for very good reasons. The processes involved in the development of the nervous system are very sensitive to alcohol. Alcohol is also one of the molecules that can get though the blood barrier of the placenta. The fetus also cannot metabolize alcohol the way the mother can, it can only get rid of it through the placenta. This means that the alcohol may be around in the fetus' body for a longer period of time.

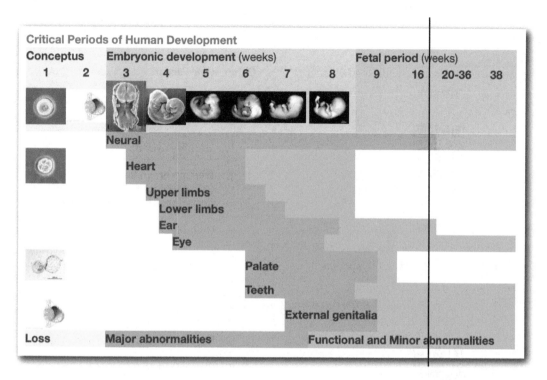

Critical Periods of Human Development

Conceptus		Embryonic development (weeks)						Fetal period (weeks)			
1	2	3	4	5	6	7	8	9	16	20-36	38

Neural

Heart

Upper limbs

Lower limbs

Ear

Eye

Palate

Teeth

External genitalia

Loss **Major abnormalities** **Functional and Minor abnormalities**

The chart above outlines periods of critical development of specific organs during early human development. Teratogens which interfere with development during the pink areas may bring about major abnormalities in that organ while those that interfere with development in the orange areas may result in function and minor abnormalities.

The example demonstrated by line indicates that a teratogen may produce major abnormalities in neurological development and functional/minor abnormalities in the ears, eyes, teeth and external genitalia

Learn more about Fetal Alcohol Syndrome Disorders (FASD)

The mechanism that is impacted the most directly from alcohol is neuron migration. This leads to an under developed cortex condition called **cortical dysplasia** which manifests when neurons fail to migrate.

MOVIE - The Story of Iyal

Other Risk Factors

Teratogens are not the only risk factors associated with prenatal development. Other factors include:

1. Mothers over 35

2. Teenage pregnancy

3. Gestational Diabetes

4. High blood pressure

5. Rh Disease

6. Weight gain

7. Stress

8. Depression

9. Paternal impact

Prenatal Assessment

Prenatal care is an essential part of the development of a healthy baby. Regular visits to your doctor and regular assessments help to identify potential problems early so early interventions can be used. Some of the typical assessments that may be employed include and **ultrasound** as well as regular blood tests.

When there is suspicion of a disorder or defect, additional assessments may be in order, including **amniocentesis** and/or **chorionic villus sampling**.

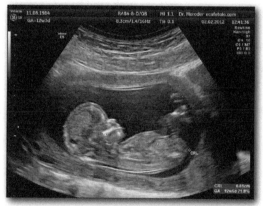

An ultrasound uses sound almost like sonar, to create a picture of the child in utero.

Childbirth

While engaged in prenatal care, you will need to make a number of decisions as to how you want to go through the birthing process. Modern medical technology available at a hospital can provide assurance to a mother going through childbirth, but many women also consider having their child at home attended by a physician or a mid-wife.

Alternative Birthing Methods

Alternative approaches to both the place and method of birthing are available. These include:

1. Having your baby at a birthing center.

2. Having your baby at home.

3. Water Births (having your baby while in a pool of water)

4. Hypnosis

5. Acupuncture and Acupressure

Read more about these at The Bump

Midwives

Throughout history, individuals within the community have gravitated toward roles to help others through their pregnancy. Midwifery has a rich cultural background of both traditional and modern medical perspectives and practices. To learn more about this fascinating and divers option for childbirth, visit the link below.

Midwives of Maine

Fathers and Birthing

Studies support that the role of fathers in the birthing process can be profound. Having a baby is one of the most important and life-changing events in a father's life. Being supporting of the mother, being present and supportive through the process, appreciating the process that mom goes through, and being present when the child enters the world are linked to both short- and long-term positive outcomes for the father, mother, and child.

Read the whole story and see more pictures!

Culture and Childbirth

Different cultures express different ideas and preferences with the process of childbirth. Living in culturally diverse areas requires that you become acquainted with the different practices of the people around you.

This topic is discussed in the Special Assignment section of this CourseBook.

How is this for a picture of both an alternative birth and a VERY involved father!

Assessment

Chapter 2 Discussion A - Traits

Reflect on specific personality or behavioral traits that you have had your entire life. Assuming that these have some sort of genetic basis, describe the trait, which parent (or ancestor) may have given you this trait, and categorize the trait on the Genotype Environment Correlations categories. Justify your choice.

Respond to others' posts by reflecting how a different Genotype Environment Correlation may have changed the outcome.

Chapter 2 Discussion B - Birthing

Discuss the pros and cons related to home child birth and other alternative birthing methods.

Chapter 2 Quiz - Critical Periods

1. A friend approaches you and tells you that while at a party she was slipped a drug in her drink. She is unsure what the drug is, but she is in her

9th week of pregnancy. She is concerned that the drug may effect the development of her unborn child. Utilizing the chart on critical periods, identify the potential impacts that this mystery drug may have on the child. Be sure to identify each area that is impacted and if the impact is potentially a "major abnormality" or a "Functional and Minor Abnormality".

2. Define what is meant by cephalocaudal development and provide an example that would be observable in a young child.

3. Define what is mean by proximodistal development and provide an example that would be observable in a young child.

Infancy and Toddlerhood

Attention

Developmental Milestones

The Center for Disease Control and Prevention publishes wonderful materials about all manner of topics, including Child Development. What should we expect week to week when our children are first born? What about year to year after that?

CENTERS FOR DISEASE
CONTROL AND PREVENTION

Topics on this site include:

- Child Development Basics

- Developmental Screening Tools

- Positive Parenting Tips

- Specific Conditions

- Developmental Milestones

- Safety

- Early Brain Development

- …and much more.

Feel free to visit this site throughout this course!

CDC - Child Development

Learning Outcomes

Upon completion of this Chapter, students should be able to:

1. Explain the benefits of myelin on the nervous system.

2. Provide an example of a concept learned through through the processes of assimilation and accommodation.

3. Discuss the importance of Erikson's first two stages on a persons development through life.

Teaching

A Popular Stage to Study

The first two years of life are a very popular age for Developmental Psychologists to study because the changes are so dynamic and important! This is also a somewhat captive audience. Children of this age (along with the next stages) are usually with families, in institutions such as childcare and school, and are thus, relatively easy to study and observe.

In this chapter we will be exploring the biological, psychological, and social clocks of the first two years!

Brain and Nervous System Development

At the time of our birth we are born with most of the 85 billion or so neurons we are going to have in our brain. From this point on, brain and nervous system development have a lot more to do with the development of additional connections between neurons.

Neurons

Let's take a look at the structure of the typical neuron so that we can identify the ways in which they develop.

The image identifies some of the basic structures of the neuron. Notably are the **dendrites**, the **axon** covered by a fatty tissue called **myelin**, and the **axon terminals** where we find **synapses**, the are of the neuron where the biochemical communicating **neurotransmitters** are activated.

The basic processes of brain and neuron development include:

1. **Dendrite Formation** - this identifies the process of the increased production of dendrites. These are physical growths from the neuron cell that appear as branches. These increase over time as a result of learning and experience and increase the number of connections between neurons.

2. **Synaptogenesis** - this identifies the process of an increase in the number of synapses (or connections) formed between neurons.

3. **Synaptic Pruning** - while the processes of dendrite formation and synaptogenesis are going on, there is another process that prunes away unused connections in order to make the brain and nervous system more efficient.

4. **Myelination** - myelin is a fatty tissue that develops on the outside of the axon over time (this process continues into childhood and when we learn new and complex activities.) Myelin plays a role in protecting and increasing the efficiency of the neuron.

By the time we are 20, we have about **100,000 miles** of myelin covered nerve fibers in our body involved in the formation of over **100 trillion synapse connections**!

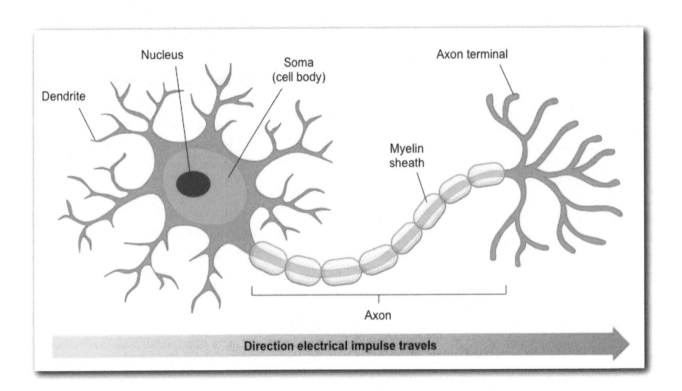

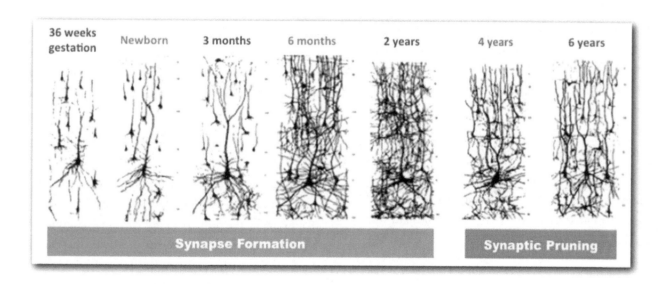

| 36 weeks gestation | Newborn | 3 months | 6 months | 2 years | 4 years | 6 years |

Synapse Formation

Synaptic Pruning

A Bit about Myelin

The fatty tissue called myelin that develops around the cells in the central and peripheral nervous system. You have likely heard the terms **grey matter** and **white matter** to describe our nervous system. Grey matter consists of the cell bodies and dendrites of the nervous system, white matter consists mostly of the axons that connect cells to each other. The white color comes from the presence of myelin. Early in life we have much less white matter than we do have grey matter.

Myelination is critical to development of increasingly complex thoughts and actions as it increases the efficiency of the nervous system. What we mean by this is speed!

Different neurons will transmit the electrical signal along the nerve at different speeds. The fastest (and most myelinated) nerves are the **alpha motor neurons** in the spinal cord which travel at a speed of **268 miles per hour!** By contrast, sensory nerve cells in the skin and eyes are relatively un-myelinated and travel a rather casual **1 mile per hour.**

The Brain

At birth the brain weighs about 25% of what an adult brain weighs. By age 2, the brain is 75% of the weight of an adult brain! Most of this growth is happening in the **cortex** which is the outer layer of the brain that is typified by the **gyrus** and **sulcus** formations we most often associate with the external appearance of the brain.

Although development is happening across the brain, different areas of the brain develop at different rates. For example, the primary motor cortex develops faster than the primary sensory cortex (it may be that the motor actions, which develop first, allow the child to move about in the environment, and thus develop their sensory systems...we will explore this later!)

Lateralization, which is the process by which particular functions become located on one half of the brain or the

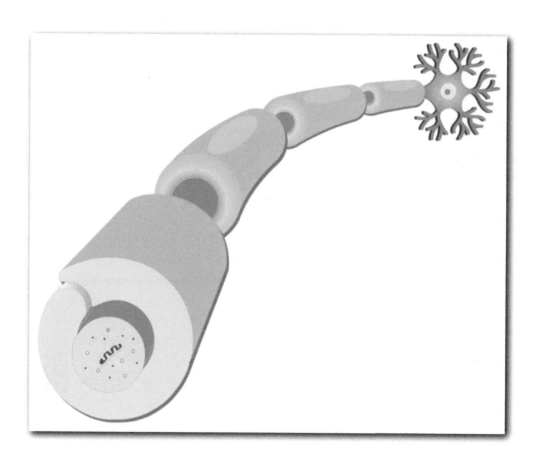

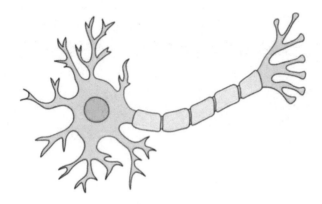

MOVIE - Myelination

other, begins to manifest during this period. In adults we know that the left hemisphere is more activated in the process of language production than the right hemisphere.

Motor Development

At birth, babies' intentional motor development is pretty limited. There are a number of **reflexes** that are common to infants. These include:

1. Sucking
2. Rooting
3. Grasp
4. Babinski
5. Moro
6. Tonic Neck
7. Stepping

Earlier we were introduced to the concept of cephalocaudal and proximodistal development. As a review, these terms describe that development occurs earlier in the head and then moves toward the tail (cephalocaudal) and from the midline to the outer limbs (proximodistal). This also applies to the sequence of gross and fine motor and sensory abilities that infants develop. Consider the illustration on the previous page.

Notice the cephalocaudal and proximodistal aspects of the stages of gross motor development. The head is raised before control of the feet (for example) and the child can roll over before they can reach up to hold themselves up.

Sensory Development

In order for our brains to develop and for us to survive we need to be able to acquire information about the world around us. Infants are born with all of their sensory capacities intact, but at different stages of devel-

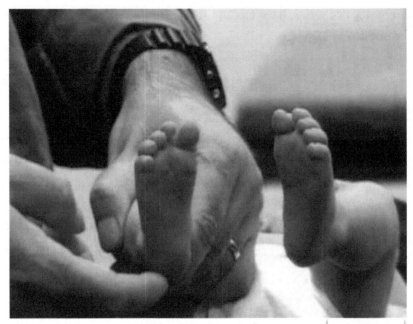

MOVIE - Newborn Reflexes

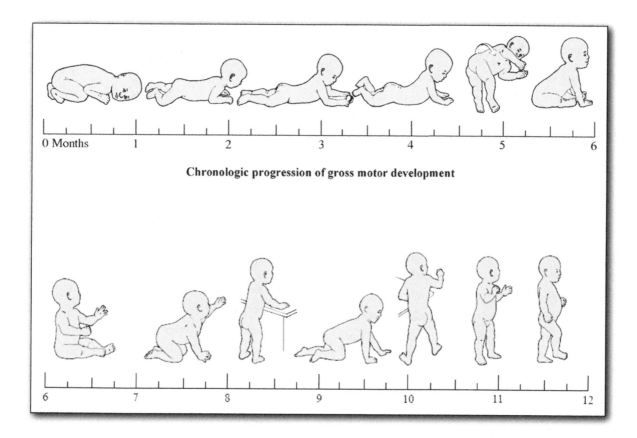

0 Months   1   2   3   4   5   6

Chronologic progression of gross motor development

6   7   8   9   10   11   12

opment because of the relatively sheltered environment of the womb during their development.

1. **Vision** - vision is the poorest developed sense because of the dark environment of the womb. The world seems very blurry to a child when they are born but they quickly adapt within the first 6 months.

It is interesting to consider that the focus point of an infant's vision is about 8-15 inches...which is well within the range of a mother's face when she is nursing. So, the baby is wired to see mom's face clearly before anything else.

2. **Hearing** - hearing is apparent by the 7th prenatal month. So, yes, your baby can hear you, your heart, and your surroundings. Infants hearing is particularly tuned to the sound spectrum of language.

Listen to the Sounds in the Womb

3. **Touch and Pain** - for a long time it was thought that infants do not feel pain (thus, procedures such as circumcision, were considered pain free). This, of course, is not true. Infants are sensitive to touch, pain, temperature, pressure, etc.

4. **Taste and Smell** - infants have been found to respond to different tastes and smells with different facial expression.

Cognitive Development and Piaget

As motor movement and sensory systems begin to develop, there are qualitative and quantitative changes going on in the brain.

We have already discussed how the brain becomes more myelinated and how neurons under dendrite formation to increase connections, but there is a qualitative aspect to this as well. One of the best known models we have about these changes in cognition early in life is from the work of Swiss Psychologist Jean Piaget.

Piaget was a prodigy having published his first several academic papers by age 15 on the subject of mollusks. His involvement with the development of one of the first intelligence tests with Alfred Binet (later to be called the Stanford-Binet Intelligence Test) sparked an interest the ways in which children come to know things.

Jean Piaget

PIAGET'S THEORY OF DEVELOPMENTAL CHANGE VIA SCHEMAS

Assimilation
(Incorporate into an existing schema)

Accommodation
(Modification of a prior schema)

EQUILIBRATION

The science of how we come to know things is called **epistemology** and the name of Piaget's theory is **Genetic Epistemology**. The term "genetic" however, does not refer to the "genes" in our cells, it is a term to describe the "genesis" or the development of our ways of knowing.

Assimilation and Accommodation

The basic processes that Piaget outlined in the development of cognition in children involve the processes of **assimilation** and **accommodation**.

1. **Assimilation** - this is the process of taking in new information and forming a thought or **schema** about the information.

2. **Accommodation** - this is the process of modifying and existing schema in order to take into account new information.

According to Piaget we **construct** our knowledge based upon experience. As we experience new things we cre-ate inner representations of them that he referred to as **schema**. As we age we are continually integrating additional schemas into our minds. At the same time we are also modifying and expanding upon these schemas as we experience things.

Consider this example of a young farmer:

This is Jim the Farmer and his son Billy-Bob Jim the Farmer has all sorts of animals on his farm and feels his son is ready to start learning about them. The first animal he shows to Billy Bob is a cow. Billy-Bob **assimilates** this new information into a basic schema he calls **cow.**

This represents the relatively immature schema of "cow" that Billy-Bob has.

Next, Jim the Farmer shows his son Billy-Bob a horse. At first, Billy-Bob notices that the horse is a lot like a cow and says "COW!" Jim the Farmer is patient with his son and says, "No, that is a horse."

At this point, Billy-Bob is undergoing two distinct processes outlined by Piaget. They including the **assimila-**tion of new information to form a schema called **horse**…

…but he is also **accommodating** new information into his existing schema of **cow** to exclude things that look like a **horse**.

At this point Billy-Bob now has two schemas, one for cow and one for horse. Both are fairly immature but as he gains experience on the farm he will continue to distinguish between these animals (and many other animals) on the farm.

The years pass by and Billy-Bob learns more and more about cows (and horses). When you ask Billy-Bob about cows NOW, this is what he thinks about.

Billy-Bob now has a **EXPERT** level schema for cow!

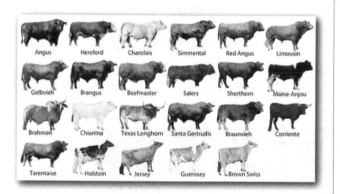

Piaget's Stages

Piaget identified qualitative changes in the way children think and conceive the world as they grow older. He found these patters and constructed a 4 part stage theory that describes cognitive development through adolescence. We will examine the first one here.

Stage 1 - Sensory-Motor

During the sensory motor stage the child is beginning to coordinate movement with sensory stimulation.

1. **Primary Circular Reactions** - at this stage, the infant is simply moving their bodies and limbs around at random. If the child happens to make something move or light up it attracts their attention and they attempt to do it again and again. This is why we hang mobiles in cribs within the grasp of small children.

2. **Secondary Circular Reactions** - at this stage the child is beginning to experiment with the

Substage 3

4 ⟶ 8 Months

...ary Circular Reactions...

moovly

MOVIE - Sensory Motor Sub-Stages

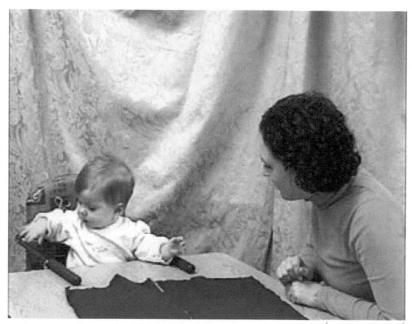

MOVIE - 7-month-old Failing Object Permanence Test

world and has some rudimentary idea as to the physical properties of objects. Balls are round and they roll and bounce, for example. They will seek out objects based on their properties. So at this stage the baby will pick up a rattle and immediately begin to shake it and they will approach a ball and immediately roll it.

3. **Tertiary Circular Reactions** - at this stage kids become quite a handful! Armed with the knowledge that balls bounce and that cats have fur and are alive...they might ask...do cats bounce? This is NEVER fun for the cat! Children at this stage start to experiment with different properties of objects, sometimes hurting or destroying them in the process. They are, according to Piaget, like little scientists.

4. **Object Permanence** - at this early stage the only reality that the child can conceive is the one that is currently in their field of perception.

When something moves out of the room or is hidden, it ceases to exist. The notion that objects (including mom!) continue to exist when they can't see them develops during this stage and they are said to have developed "object permanence."

Language Development

Language is a system of communication that uses symbols in a regular way to create meaning. Language is one of the most significant differences between us and the rest of the animal kingdom, as far as we can tell. While other animals use sounds that have meaning, our language capacity is constructive. We can continually rearrange sounds to create infinite varieties of meaning.

As a child is developing language, they go through a number of different stages:

Episode 16

LANGUAGE

MOVIE - Language

1. Newborns communicate through body movements, facial expressions, and sounds (such as crying).

2. **Cooing** is comprised of the one syllable sounds combinations of a vowel and consonant such a "ba" or "coo" This process serves as an internal feedback system for the baby who is beginning to integrate motor movement (in this case the tongue and mouth) with sensory experience (hearing).

3. At about 7 months children begin to **babble**. The difference is that we begin to pick up on inflections in the voice much as if they understand what they are trying to say, but the choice of sounds is not recognizable.

4. **Gesturing** is used to communicate as well. Pointing to things communicates that they want you to get it for them.

5. Understanding of language, **receptive language**, precedes the ability to produce language. Children are able to understand more words than they can produce.

6. At about 12 months babies can produce understandable words. These words tend to have **holophrasis** qualities in that the single word means more than simply the name of an object. A baby may say "cookie" and we interpret this (by reading facial expressions and body movements) that they are saying "I want a cookie."

7. Predictable **language errors** indicate some of the internal processing that is happening when it comes to learning language. Confusing consonant sounds and the under-extension (a word only means a specific object) and overextension (a word begins to label all objects that are similar to the original object) of words. Within this

you are seeing the active construction of cognitive schemas for these objects.

8. Two word sentences begin to emerge as toddlers. Much of the grammar is not yet intact, however, and phrases such as "Doggie eats" may mean "The dog is eating."

9. Infant directed speech is the universal tendency by adults to use a higher frequency voice and exaggerations in tone and word. We call this **motherese** and these vocalizations convey as much meaning in the **tone** as they do in the actual words being used.

MOVIE - Motherese

Theories of Language Development

The three major approaches to how we learn language are behavioral, social cognitive, and nativistic.

1. **Behavioral** - this theory supports that while the child begins to make sounds certain sounds are identified by the environment and reinforced with attention and excitement from the people in the child's environment. Over time, the utterances are shaped into what we know as language.

2. **Social Cognitive** - this model supports the notion that children observe, imitate, and are reinforces for utterances that closely approximate language.

3. **Nativistic** - this model was developed by the world renowned linguist, Noam Chomsky. He recognized that the behavioral and social cognitive approaches could not explain the common errors that children make when learning to

Noam Chomsky

These days Noam Chomsky is very active in the political and public dialogue regarding social justice, media, and the current political climate. He
is one of the greatest thinkers of the age and worthy of exploration.

Website

MOVIE - Noam Chomsky's Language Acquisition Device

Wernicke's Area

- Location
- **Left Temporal lobe**
- Major function:
- **It is important for the comprehension of speech sounds and is considered to be the language comprehension, centre.**

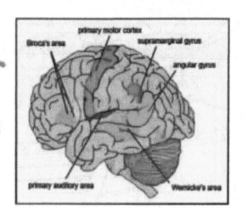

MOVIE - Broca's and Wernicke's Areas and Aphasias ——

—— Website with video examples of both Broca's and Wernicke's Area Aphasia

Language & The Brain

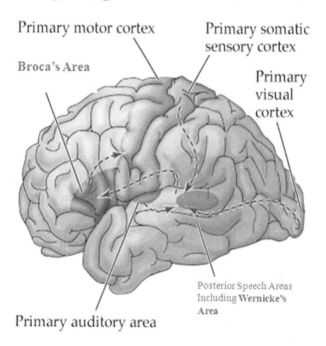

Primary motor cortex

Primary somatic sensory cortex

Broca's Area

Primary visual cortex

Posterior Speech Areas Including **Wernicke's** Area

Primary auditory area

speak. In particular were the errors associated with syntax, such as attaching the -ed to a word to set it in the past. Small children tend to overextend these rules and utter phrases such as "I falled down" or "He goed to the store."

Chomsky's Language Acquisition Device

While it is likely that the name of this theory is poorly constructed, Chomsky refers here to a number of brain areas that are innately tuned to learn and apply the rules (syntax) of language. Humans enter the world with the LAD and other animals do not, and Chomsky supports that is why humans have complex language and other animals do not.

A bit-o-Biology

Some actual structures in the brain have been identified as specifically associated with language. Paul Broca (1824-1880) was on the forefront of developing techniques for mapping functions across the cortex of the human brain. Upon conducting the autopsies on two of his patients who suffered from language impairment, he noted structural damage to the part of the brain that now bears his name **Broca's Area**.

Carl Wernicke theorized that another part of the brain was also involved in language and **Wernicke's Area** now bears his name.

Early Personality

Temperament

One of the first indications of "personality" in an infant is referred to as **temperament**. Temperament represents the innate characteristics of an infant, including mood, activity level, and emotional reactivity, noticeable soon after birth. The classic New York Longitudinal Study revealed a set of temperament types:

1. **Easy** (40%) - baby is able to adapt to new situations easily, remains calm, is easy to sooth, and is usually in a positive mood.

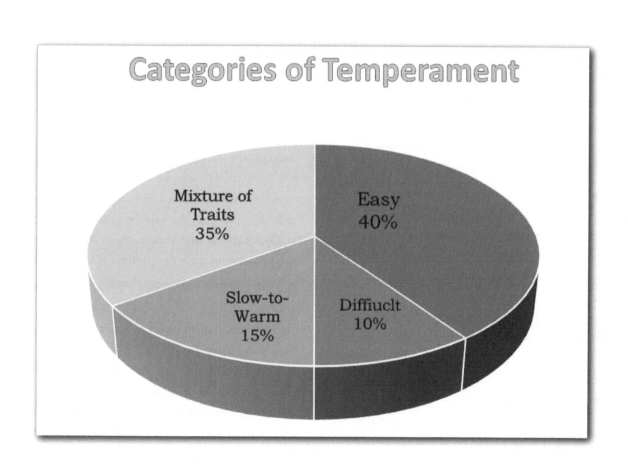

2. **Difficult** (10%) - reacts negatively to new situations, has trouble adapting to routines, is usually in a negative mood, and cries frequently.

3. **Slow-to-Warm Up** (15%) - baby has a low activity level, adjusts slowly to new situations and is often in a negative mood.

This categorization of early personality has been critiqued for its use of the terms "easy" and "difficult." It is important to recognize that while different babies show different behavior patterns, the personality of the adults in the room are important factors in the interaction as well. **Goodness of Fit** is the term that describes the degree to which a baby's personality matches the personality, preferences, and expectations of the parent. If there is a high level of match (excitable, outgoing, adventurous) between both the parent and the child, things go more smoothly!

Attachment and Trust

As the child develops they encounter relationships with others in their world. These interactions contribute to the psychosocial development of the child.

Attachment is a close bond with the caregiver through which the child develops a sense of security. We discussed **Goodness of Fit** earlier and this plays a role in attachment as well. As does the presence or absence of any **Postpartum Depression**. Since attachment is so closely linked to these first feelings of security, this process if vital.

When my children were born I had a number of conversations with all the people we met at the hospital. Being a social worker at the time I was interested in attachment and how the hospital identified at-risk kids. At-risk refers to the notion that the children may be neglected or be at risk for other issues. Social workers were automatically assigned to a family if any of the following was present:

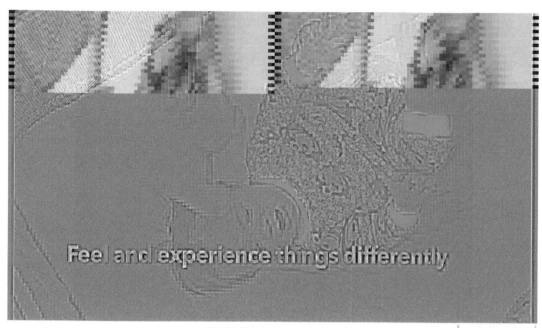

Feel and experience things differently

MOVIE - Temperament

MOVIE - Strange Situation Test showing

Secure Attachment

1. Disability (physical or sensory)

2. Premature Birth

3. Postpartum Depression

4. Difficulties with Attachment

5. Cleft Lip

The last one struck me as interesting. The social worker stated that when a child has a cleft lip a number of things may happen. For one, the child may have difficulty nursing and thus they are at risk for malnutrition. In addition, a mother, having gone through a lot of pain and discomfort, often overcomes these feelings when they nurse their child. Attachment happens and life is off to a good start.

A child with a cleft lip may have attachment issues and thus the mom is more likely to have postpartum as well.

Another sad reality is this. When I talked with the photographer who took Hannah's first picture, he told me that he has been taking pictures of newborns for over 20 years and he has never been asked to take a picture of a baby with a cleft lip. The parents have always opted to not have pictures done.

Attachment Theory

John Bowlby and Mary Ainsworth developed a now famous methodology for studying the attachment between a child and their caregiver. From this methodology they observed four different types of attachment. The method is referred to as the **Strange Situation Test**.

Attachment Styles

Secure Attachment

Believes and trusts that his needs will be met

MOTHER
Quick
Sensitive
Consistant

CHILD
Secure
Exploring
Happy

Avoidant Attachment

MOTHER
Distant
Disengaged

CHILD
Not very explorative
Emotionally distant

Subconsciously believes that his needs probably won't be met

Ambvivalent Attachment

Cannot rely on his needs to be met

MOTHER
Inconsistent
Sometimes sensitive
Sometimes neglectful

CHILD
Anxious
Insecure
Angry

Disorganized Attachment

Severely confused with no strategy to have his needs met

MOTHER
Extreme
Frightened
Frightening
Passive

CHILD
Depressed
Passive
Angry
Non-responsive

www.AttachFromScratch.com

The Attachment Project

This website provides information on how early attachment style impacts later relationships. The site contains a test you can take to assess your current attachment style!

The Attachment Project

Attachment and Bonding

Since we are talking about attachment that happens so early in life, it is a good time to talk about bonding as well. Both involve an emotional connection that is created between two people. In most cases we identify this as the attachment that occurs between a child and their caregiver.

Attachment occurs over time. We grow "attached" and used to the familiarity of persons. We may become attached to other things as well, because they are familiar and comfortable. Bonding is different.

Bonding is a sense of connection that can occur that is immediate and emotionally profound. Sometimes the bond may be fleeting such as in the sense of connection we might have to those around us at a concert as we enjoy an artist we mutually admire.

Some bonds may more long lasting and occur due to shared experience, even trauma. Individuals who survived the attack on the World Trade Center on September 11, 2001 have an emotional bond with each other that will likely last the rest of their lives. They may not even continually like each other! Yet that connection will still be there. Brothers and sisters in combat is similar.

Positive events can also bring about bonding such as members of a winning team, our high school class, our peer group in college, etc.

We are designed to create lasting connections with others through both processes of attachment and bonding throughout our lives. There is even a type of bonding called **Trauma Bonding**. Unlike my previous example, this is demonstrated by the emotional bond that is created between an abuser and their target. It grows around the cycle of abuse, devaluation, and positive reinforcement. In these circumstances, it is useful to seek help sorting out the powerful emotions involved.

Erik Erikson

One of my favorite theories in all of Developmental Psychology is the theory of Erik Erikson.

Erik Erikson

Erikson was a student of Sigmund Freud, but disagreed with Freud on a number of points...particularly on two of them...

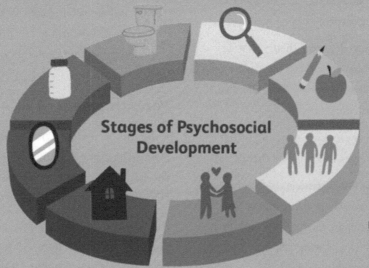

Stages of Psychosocial Development

Infancy
trust vs. mistrust

Early Childhood
autonomy vs. shame and doubt

Preschool
initiative vs. guilt

School Age
industry vs. inferiority

Adolescence
identity vs. role confusion

Young Adulthood
intimacy vs. isolation

Middle Adulthood
generativity vs. stagnation

Maturity
ego integrity vs. despair

1. Humans developed through **psychosocial** stages of development, not **psychosexual** stages.

2. Development happened across the **lifespan**, it did not end at adolescence.

Like Piaget, Erikson developed a stage theory that describes a series of tasks to be worked out between the developing psyche (mind) and society (hence the term "psychosocial" that Erikson developed.)

In our current chapter we are looking at the ages that accompany the first two stages in Erikson's theory.

1. **Trust vs. Mistrust** - at this stage the child is absolutely dependent on their environment for survival. Does the environment want and provide for the child? During this first year, there is no such thing as "spoiling" a child. Responding to every cry and every laugh (as much as possible) ensures that the child will learn to trust the world and its ability to sustain him.

2. **Autonomy vs. Shame and Doubt** - we might equate this to the "terrible twos." Children are moving about in the world during the 2nd year and are getting into all kinds of mischief. They are also learning to act in the world. We need to support safe exploration and provide these opportunities.

Parenting and...Autonomy

Autonomy supporting parenting practices move away from strict authoritarian and permissive practices. Authoritative parenting, a balance of high affection and appropriate control, is ideal.

At this stage, parents are trying to instill in their children a sense of autonomy. Adult autonomy expresses itself as the process of critical thinking. We look at our options, evaluate our best course of action, and select our next steps.

To encourage these skills in your child:

- Provide unconditional love.

- Give your child the opportunity to make age-ap-propriate decisions.

- Help your child feel valued and competent.

- Demonstrate empathy and employ active listening skills.

Read more about Autonomy Supportive Parenting by visiting this website.

What is Autonomy Supportive Parenting
and How to Practice it

Assessment

Chapter 3 Discussion - Trust

Stages 1 and 2 of Erikson's theory are foundational and can shape much of the way of a persons' life from that point on. Consider the importance of trust and autonomy in adult life. Discuss the potential impacts of successful and unsuccessful trust and autonomy on adulthood.

In addition, consider your Attachment Style as indicated in the test available from the Attachment Project. How does this reflect in your current relationships?

Chapter 3 Quiz - Myelination + Piaget

1. Describe the process of myelination and why it is necessary for the development of complex coordinated activity such as walking, running, and dancing.

2. Reflect on all the things you have learned. Write an example of how you learned about something

Early Childhood

4

Attention

Parenting

Although the monetary pay is really poor, parenting is probably the most important job that exists. \As we enter the study of Early Childhood we would do well to take a look at how our expectation for parenting anyhow we care for our children may need to be revised.

The Tragic Decline of Bored Kids
and Dangerous Play

Learning Outcomes

Upon completion of this Chapter, students should be able to:

1. Apply an understanding of Theory of Mind to an analysis of a case study.

2. Outline early and late life indicators of a person's transition through the first three stages of Erikson's Psychosocial Theory.

3. Explore perspective regarding non-binary gender identity.

Teaching

Growth and Development

Children between the ages of 2 and 6 tend to grow about 3 inches in height and about 4-5 pounds in weight a year.

View the CDC Growth Charts

For proper growth and development, children aged 2-3 need about 1000 to 1400 calories and children ages 4-8 need 1200 to 2000 calories per day.

Brain Maturation

The brain is about 75% of its adult weight by the time we are three years old. Myelination and dendritification continue through this stage. There is a noted development in the left hemisphere related to language development and in the right hemisphere related to spatial skills.

We will begin to see changes in play behavior that reflect the development in the prefrontal cortex. This part of the brain is responsible for thinking, developing strategies, and for managing emotions.

Motor Development

This is a rather intense time of motor development. Children learn to run, skip, jump, climb and all sorts of other activities. Your text has an excellent chart similar to this one.

As with all things, there is an interaction between the developing body and nervous system and the environment. Children need to be able to play and explore in order to develop these skills.

Sports in Early Childhood

Playing sports in early childhood has many beneficial effects:

1. Better vision
2. Healthy weight
3. Motor skill development
4. Social skill development
5. Self-confidence
6. Sportsmanship
7. Fun and enjoyment
8. Friendship

Professional athletes have long been known for their very early start in their respective sport.

Changes in Gross- and Fine-Motor Skills During Early Childhood

Age	Gross-Motor Skills	Fine-Motor Skills
2–3 years	• Jumps, hops, throws, and catches with rigid upper body • Pushes riding toy with feet; little steering	• Puts on and removes simple items of clothing • Uses large zippers • Uses spoon effectively
3–4 years	• Jumps and hops, flexing upper body • Throws and catches with slight upper-body involvement • Pedals and steers tricycle	• Fastens and unfastens large buttons • Serves self food without help • Uses scissors • Draws first picture of person
4–5 years	• Runs more smoothly • Gallops and skips • Throws with increased body rotation	• Uses fork effectively • Cuts with scissors following line • Copies shapes and some letters
5–6 years	• Increases running speed • Mature throwing, catching • Rides bicycle with training wheels	• Uses knife • Ties shoes • Draws more detailed person • Copies numbers and simple words

PEARSON

Tiger Woods performed a swing on the Mike Douglas show at age 2

Shawn White was professionally sponsored in snow-boarding at age 10

Serena Williams began to play tennis at age 4

Dorothy Hamill started taking her skating seriously at age 8 in 1965, going to the ice rink every morning at 4:30 am to practice before school. This picture is of her in 1976 winning her first Gold Medal in the Olympics.

Here is what the experts say...

1. While it seems that the key to professional success in sports may be to start very young, parents what to be cautious about entering their young children in competitive sports early.

2. Sports like swimming and gymnastics can be excellent sources of exercise and fun for kids as young as 2 years old.

3. Children are generally not ready for competitive sports until ages 5 or 6.

4. Many of the athletes mentioned above were gifted and presented an unusual dedication and commitment. Many children will simply be children and wander from sport to sport. If your child is one of the gifted and dedicated ones, simply nurture it...if not, just keep the early sports fun.

Cognitive Development

Piaget's Schemas and Operations

Before we go on to the next stage, we have to explore the concept of schemas and operations. Schemas we have already covered. Operations describe the ability to sustain representations of the objects and are able to "manipulate" or think about these objects in their minds. From this point on, Piaget's theory focuses on these "operations" or the ability to conceive and manipulate objects.

Stage 2 - Pre-operational

As the name implies, this stage exists prior to the ability to hold objects in one's mind. The world is still represented by what the child himself is perceiving and they possess **cognitive egocentrism**, which is to say, that they feel that others see what they see. Unable to manipulate and reverse actions they see in the real world, Piaget developed a number of ingenious ways to observe the typical mistakes that a child in the pre-operational stage would make.

1. **Conservation** - children are still learning about the constancies of physical properties in the world. They are NOT able to conserve matter in the pre-operational stage and they make mistakes related to how objects change shape and arrangement.

2. **Egocentrism** - children still relate to the world from their own perspective and do not understand that others have different thoughts and viewpoints as they do (they have not developed "Theory of Mind," discussed later). This is not a personality problem, at least not at this age! But they will assume others see reality as they do.

Another aspects of cognitive development that appear during this stage involve the onset of **symbolic function** or the development of language to represent objects. This function develops over time through repeated association between sounds and objects. **Animism** is the characteristic of this stage of development where human characteristics are assumed to exist in animals and objects. A doll, for instance can be hurt and feel emotions.

MOVIE - Mountain Task

MOVIE - Conservation Tasks

COGNITIVE DEVELOPMENT

SENSORIMOTOR

BIRTH - 2 YEARS

PREOPERATIONAL

2 - 7 YEARS

CONCRETE OPERATIONAL

7 - 12 YEARS

FORMAL OPERATIONAL

12 YEARS ONWARD

Information Process

While Piaget's work tends to focus on the **qualitative** aspects of thinking and cognition, the Information Processing model focuses research on **quantifiable** aspects of cognitive development such as memory, attention, and language development.

Attention

Key to learning is the ability to attend to stimuli. It is the first step in the process of memory formation and key for our sense organs to receive and transmit information to our brains. Measures of **divided attention** (the ability to switch from task to task - we don't multi-task), **selective attention** (focusing on a specific aspect of the environment and actively ignoring other stimuli, and **sustained attention** or **attention span** (the duration of our ability to engage in selective attention) are key areas of development of interest to educators and psychologists alike.

1. 3-5 year olds have much difficulty with divided attention.

2. Selective attention improves with age but this is greatly influenced by the child's temperament, the complexity of the task, and the type of stimuli (visual or auditory.) Among most children, visual stimuli bring about greater selective attention than does auditory stimuli. This is particular true if the environments have background noise. Children have great difficulty separating the teacher's voice from other sounds.

3. Sustained attention, as well, gets better with age.

As can be seen in this table, depending on the type of activity, mixing up presentation style, learning activity, and movement are important aspects of the learning environment of young children.

Age	Attention Span
1 year	3-5 minutes
2 year	4-10 minutes
3 year	6-15 minutes
4 year	8-20 minutes
5 year	10-25 minutes
6 year	12-30 minutes

Consider your role at work with children and a need you have to teach them something. How might you change your approach based on the age of the child?

Memory

Before we take on memory development, let's review the memory process.

Several processes are involved in the formation and retrieval of memories. Each of these have their own independent developmental pathway.

1. Sensory memory is quite fragile and is the most subject to differences in attention span. New and novel images help attract the attention of young children.

2. Working memory changes over time with 5 year olds able to handle about 5 things in short term memory.

3. The most salient issue is that the selective attention and rehearsal processes in memory are intentional. This means the child has to be engaged in the purposeful activity of creating memories (sort of like studying.) This entails a degree of **executive functioning** and development in the prefrontal cortex (discussed earlier.)

4. A child who is an environment that is warm and responsive, uses scaffolding (see Vygotsky) when problem solving with the child, and provides cognitively stimulating activities show higher executive functioning at an earlier age. This is really the key factor involved in having children live and experience these types of environments.

Lev Vygotsky

Vygotsky was a Russian psychologist who focused on the cultural and social interactionist aspects of cognitive development. While he did not disagree with Piaget that the child had innate qualities that led to cognitive development, Vygotsky's work identified ways in which

ANXIETY ZONE

ZONE OF

COMFORT ZONE

what you can
already do
by yourself

PROXIMAL DEVELOPMENT

what you can't do

the child interacts with the environment in order to develop.

Lev Vygotsky

Zone of Proximal Development

Vygotsky felt that the best way for development to happen (learning) was when we were in a social situation with more expert others, either teachers or peers. We interacted with those individuals in such a way as to learn and develop from them. In essence, they helped us.

When we are learning a given task, we have a degree of ability to do parts of it independently, parts that we can do with help, and still other parts we can't do at all yet. The area of our ability that is just beyond our ability to do alone is what Vygotsky called the **Zone of Proximal Development**. This is where the learning occurred. We just needed a little help to get through that step.

The implications of this concept for teaching is obvious. Teachers strive to remain in the "zone" without being too easy or too hard. This is challenging when there is a room full of people at different developmental levels.

MOVIE - Roxanne's Private Speech

Scaffolding

Scaffolding was discussed in the section on memory. Scaffolding is related to the concept of the ZPD. Teachers who engage students within the ZPD are the "scaffold" that allows them to acquire the next stage of independent development and shift the zone to a higher level of independence. The skill is to provide just enough help to the student to get them to do the behavior as independently as possible.

Private Speech

Another concept put forth by Vygotsky was the concept of **Private Speech**. Vygotsky noticed that people of all ages develop the ability to talk themselves through the steps of a task. While we may call it muttering or a distraction, Vygotsky saw it as a validation of his theory.

We are so in need of social interaction to learn that in the absence of others, we will simply talk to ourselves! In some instances this has been directly applied to teaching method where students are instructed to talk themselves through a task!

Theory of Mind

One of the most important milestones in cognitive development that a child goes through at this stage is the development of **Theory of Mind**. This ability is continually developing but usually appears at around age 3.

Theory of Mind is the knowledge that others see the world from their own perspective and thus do not share your perspective of the world. At a young age this is largely expressed in terms of sensory information and is linked to the pre-operational stage from Piaget, exemplified in the mountain task.

Characteristics of Theory of Mind

1. **Diverse Desires** - understanding that two people may have different desires regarding the same object.

To test of someone has Theory of Mind, the following can be shown a child,

The child being tested knows that Anne has moved the ball from the basket to the box. If the child **DOES NOT** have Theory of Mind they will assume Sallie knows this as well and will say that Sallie looks in the box. If the child **DOES** have Theory of Mind they will know that Sallie did not see that Anne moved the ball, and that Sallie will look first at the place where Sallie put it.

2. **Diverse Beliefs** - understanding that two people may hold different beliefs about an object.

3. **Knowledge Access** - understanding that people may or may not have access to information.

4. **False Belief** - understanding that someone might hold a different belief based on false information.

5. **Hidden Emotions** - understanding that people may not always express true emotions.

Identity Development and Erikson

Throughout this period of development, children develop an increasingly complex concept of the world. They also develop an increasingly complex concept of themselves!

Through this stage we move quickly from the period where the child does not even recognize objects to exist when they can't experience them all the way to the development of self concept and the self esteem. This is a busy stage!

In these early years we begin to see the development of such schemas as:

1. **Self-concept** - how one would describe themselves.

2. **Self-esteem** - the perception as their own acceptance and value.

3. **Self-control** - the ability to manage physical and emotional actions.

4. **Gender Roles** - the behaviors and tasks that are linked to gender and cultural norms, values, and expectations (discussed below).

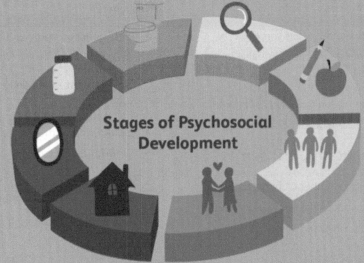

Early Childhood
autonomy vs. shame and doubt

Preschool
initiative vs. guilt

Infancy
trust
vs.
mistrust

School Age
industry
vs.
inferiority

Stages of Psychosocial
Development

Maturity
ego integrity
vs.
despair

Adolescence
identity
vs.
role confusion

Middle Adulthood
generativity vs. stagnation

Young Adulthood
intimacy vs. isolation

Initiative vs Guilt

In our current chapter we are looking at the ages that accompany the third stage in Erikson's theory.

Initiative vs. Guilt - many parents will tell you that the "terrible twos" are nothing compared to the "terrifying threes!" At this point, the child has learned quite a bit about the world, understands roles and expectations in the household. This is the child that may take it upon themselves to make breakfast for the family some early morning!

As with all of Erikson's stages, the supportive environment is critical to nurturing a positive outcome. The stages we have examined so far include: Trust vs. Mistrust, Autonomy vs. Shame and Doubt, and now Initiative vs. Guilt. Extreme negative outcomes in these three stages often lead to profoundly compromised functioning in the person. These first three stages set the stage for self-concepts that will last a lifetime.

Parenting and...Initiative

This can be one of the more frustrating times for parents as their children begin to take more control over aspects of their daily lives. Remember, one major goal of parenting is to create the capacity to initiate action, you can do this!

During this state, as we will explore next, children begin to play with others and they begin to sense that individuals have roles to play. This is similar to the observations they have made at home regarding activities in the household. Demonstrating and talking about roles in the household help to reinforce these ideas about how people work together to accomplish different goals.

This is ALSO the time to address notions of gender roles specific to duties around the house! If you want your son to do his own laundry and you want your daughter to work on the car, now is the time to demonstrate this!

Helping your child explore leadership, planning, and carrying out plans in their play encourages initiative. These opportunities can also be found in chores around the house by inviting the children to participate in the shared responsibility of the household.

Imaginary friends may emerge during this stage. This is a safe and normal way for children to experiment with the emerging skills they are developing to initiate and control social situations. This is not a mental illness! Most children know the difference between their imaginary friends and the real people around them.

Initiating and leading is a new skill. Some kids might be more assertive or bossy than others. It is important to address this by helping children learn to be cooperative leaders. Being able to negotiate and take others' perspective into consideration is beginning to emerge during this period (see Theory of Mind) and should be encouraged!

According to Erikson, the complementary outcome of this stage is "guilt". Parents who restrict their child's participation in play groups or are overprotective when it comes to conflict in this groups are keeping their children away from opportunities to learn how to resolve differences among their peers. While it might seem like you are keeping your child away from harm, you may actually be creating as sense of guilt regarding their own abilities to navigate the social world.

While we don't encourage "guilt trips" a little bit of guilt when a child has crossed a line with a playmate or family member is a good thing. When they make mistakes, it is appropriate to model how to apologize and rebuild the relationship. This also encourages perspective taking and supports effective initiative, leadership, and social interaction.

Play

One of the most important aspects of a child's life where much of these cognitive and social situations are learned are within the context of play. Children spend a great deal of time at play. Both Piaget and Vygotsky saw play as a critical element of cognitive development.

At the sam time, the type of play that children engage in reflects the complexity of the cognitive, language, and social development. It is a fact that most of the theories that you have learned in this chapter have been studied through detailed observations of children at play!

Types of Play

Unoccupied Play

Unoccupied play refers to activity when a child actually isn't playing at all. He may be engaged in seemingly random movements, with no objective. Despite appearances, this definitely is play and sets the stage for future play exploration.

Solitary Play

Solitary play is just what it sounds like—when your child plays alone. This type of play is important because it teaches a child how to keep himself entertained, eventually setting the path to being self-sufficient. Any child can play independently, but this type of play is the most common in younger children around ages 2 or 3. At that age, they are still pretty self-centered and lack good communication skills. If a child is on the shy side and doesn't know his playmates well, he may prefer this type of play.

Onlooker Play

Onlooker play is when a child simply observes other children playing and doesn't partake in the action. It's common for younger children who are working on their developing vocabulary. Don't worry if your little one is behaving this way. It could be that the child feels shy, needs to learn the rules, or maybe is the youngest and wants just to take a step back for a while.

Parallel Play

Put two 3-year-olds in a room together and this is what you are likely to see: the two children having fun, playing side by side in their own little world. It doesn't mean that they don't like one another, they are just engaging in parallel play. Despite having little social contact between playmates, children who parallel play actually learn quite a bit from one another like taking turns and other social niceties. Even though it appears they aren't paying attention to each other, they truly are and often mimic the other one's behavior. As such, this type of play is viewed as an important bridge to the later stages of play.

Associative Play

Slightly different from parallel play, associative play also features children playing separately from one another. But in this mode of play, they

are involved with what the others are doing—think children building a city with blocks. As they build their individual buildings, they are talking to one another and engaging each other. This is an important stage of play because it helps little ones develop a whole host of skills—socialization (what should we build now?) and problem solving (how can we make this city bigger?), cooperation (if we work together we can make our city even better) and language development (learning what to say to get their messages across to one another). Through associative play is how children begin to make real friendships.

Cooperative Play

Cooperative play is where all the stages come together and children truly start playing together. It is common in older preschoolers or in younger preschoolers who have older siblings or have been around a lot of children). Cooperative play uses all of the social skills your child has been working on and puts them into action. Whether they are building a puzzle together, playing a board game, or enjoying an outdoor group game, cooperative play sets the stage for future interactions as your child matures into an adult.

Dramatic Fantasy Play

When your child who loves to play dress up, doctor, or restaurant, it's dramatic or fantasy play. Through this type of play, not only does your child's imagination get a workout, but she learns how to take turns, cooperate, share and work on language development. Through role-play, kids are also able to learn about functioning in the greater community.

Competitive Play

Whether she's beating her brother at Chutes and Ladders or playing on a local soccer team, your child is engaging in competitive play. Rules and turn-taking, and functioning as part of a team are the big lessons taken from this type of play. You may have to give your child guidance about dealing with both winning and losing.

Physical Play

Gross and fine motor skills really come into play here, whether your child is throwing a ball or riding a bike. Physical play encourages kids to be active.

Constructive Play

Forms of constructive play include building with blocks, making a road for toy cars, or constructing a fort out of couch pillows. Constructive play teaches kids about manipulation, building, and fitting things together. Cognitive skills are used to figure out how to make something work best, whether it is a block tower that won't stand up or a sand castle that keeps collapsing.

Symbolic Play

This type of play can be vocal (singing, jokes, rhymes), graphic arts (drawing, coloring), counting, or making music. This type of play helps children learn to develop skills in expressing themselves and exploring their experiences, ideas, and emotions.

Check out this article about television!

It's OK if your Kids are getting more Screen Time

Gender Development

Gender is a hot topic in our society. In the past, the concepts of "gender" and "sex" were nearly interchangeable, even though they always meant different things. The term "sex" is meant to identify the biological component, the genetic component of male and female. Gender has always referenced culturally defined norms, values, and expectations about males and females.

When we are born, we are each assigned a sex (female or male) based upon our anatomy, and a gender (woman or man) based upon our sex. When a person experiences distress over the gender and/or sex they were assigned at birth, that person may be suffering from **gender dysphoria.** This means that their gender identity - their sense of themselves as woman, man, or another gender entirely - is mismatched with their assigned sex (biology) and/or assigned gender (the values, norms, and expectations associated with the terms woman and man.)

Most people are **cisgender** which is to say tat their identity corresponds with the sex and gender assignments that occurred at birth. **Transgender** people, however, can experience intense distress at the incongruence between a gender identity that is at odds with their assigned gender and/or sex. **Non-binary** people (who are often included under the "trans umbrella") experience a gender identity that does not fit within the traditional "binary" models of man and woman.

Gender Roles Socialization is the process by which a culture teaches children about the "appropriate" behaviors for males and females. These have largely been exclusive one another for a lot of human history. In today's world, particularly in the West, these differences are becoming less distinct.

The concept of **gender identity** is not new, though it is more prevalent in the public consciousness that it was before.. Gender identity refers to the concept that of the options available, a person may feel aligned with the cultural expectations of maleness and femaleness that match their biological sex or not. One question that psychology has attempted to address is the degree to which a person's experience of this represents a mental disorder (as in older diagnoses, such as the DSM-4's "Gender Identity Disorder") or gender diversity (as in the DSM-5's current "Gender Dysphoria".)

It is critical to recognize that a "diagnosis" such as "Gender Dysphoria" presumes that the individual experiences distress. Categories and diagnoses in the DSM are not always listed because they are perceived as conditions that need to be "fixed". This is the case with Gender Dysphoria. However, persons who experience intense distress that interferes with their functioning can be "diagnosed" with Gender Dysphoria and receive services to address their distress (which may include counseling, support, social change, family education, and advocacy.)

Note that another reason for items to be included in the DSM is to spark research. Much of the funds available for research insist that the "condition" to be researched needs to be validated in the field and inclusion in the DSM is a way that this demand is met.

Often, trans people will undergo social transition (changing their name, pronouns, clothing, etc.) and/or medical transition (hormone therapy, sexual reassignment surgeries, etc.) to align their social identity and their bodies with their gender identity.

Providing resources that validate the notion of transgender or non-binary identity can go a long way toward helping an individual feel connected to a community that supports their personal expression.

The LGBTQ+ community advocates for a more accepting definition of gender that normalizes the unique sets of identities that we have. Through advocacy for the use of specific gender definitions and personal pronouns, people seek to create an environment that de marginalizes individuals or lessens the distress caused by the narrow views of what it means to be a woman or a man.

For some, the notion of trans or nonbinary gender identity may be unfamiliar. Various cultures in the world, and throughout history, have recognized additional words to describe other genders aside from "male" and "female".

The American Psychological Association (APA) has established specific guidelines for psychologists working with persons who are transgender or gender-non-conforming.

APA Guidelines for Psychological Practice with Transgender and Gender Non-conforming People

For some individuals, the notion of gender, and its ties to specific behavior, clothes, and looks, is particular fluid. In this video, Audrey Mason-Hyde reveals their experiences on a day-to-day basis and how the world is experienced by a gender-fluid person.

Persons interested in learning more about LGTBQ+ can start at the University of Maine's Rainbow Resource Center.

The reality is that transgender and nonbinary gender identity remains, for many, controversial. We, as a college community, aspire to support all individuals in their quest to be and express themselves as they are.

Another great resource for understanding gender related identities is the "gender bread person".

The Genderbread Person

A graphic representation of the diversity of identity

VIDEO - Toilets, Bowties, Gender, and Me

Assessment

Chapter 4 Discussion - Gender ID

Review the resources that are found at the end of the Chapter regarding trans and nonbinary gender identity. Post comments regarding something that you may have learned that you did know before.

Remember that our discussions are always kind and supportive.

Chapter 4 Quiz - Fido

Use this story to answer the question in the quiz.

Sallie was playing with her dog Fido in the living room.

Her mother was in the kitchen, out of sight, washing dishes.

Sallie jumped on the couch which slid and knocked over a table lamp which crashed to the floor. Mom ran in to make sure Sallie was OK. Once she was sure that Sallie was safe, she gave a stern look at Sallie and asked,

"What happened?" Sallie thought for a while and then stated, "Fido knocked the lamp off the table."

From this story we KNOW that Sallie has developed Theory of Mind.

1. Based on the story of Sallie and Fido the dog, explain why we can be sure that Sallie has Theory of Mind.

Chapter 4 Assignment - Erikson

Purpose

The purpose of this assignment is to enable you to apply an understanding of early psychosocial development to the interpretation of stories of early childhood from others. Being able to connect early life experiences with milestones in development are important in understanding the impact of those early experiences of later life.

Skills and Knowledge

You will demonstrate the following skills and knowledge by completing this assignment:

1. Interview and questioning skills with your subject.

2. Understanding of Erikson's first three stages (Trust vs Mistrust, Autonomy vs Doubt, and Initiative vs Guilt.)

3. Write a title page and paper in a word processor.

4. Outline early and late life indicators of a person's transition through the first three stages of Erikson's Psychosocial Theory.

5. Relate early experiences to functioning in later life.

6. Upload the paper to the assignment drop box.

Task

For this assignment you are going to report out on some stories from the early childhood of your subject in the Biography. We are looking to make connections to early childhood stories (first three years), Erikson's first three stages, and later development.

Interview your subject about these first three years. Their recollection may be more about what they have been told and may be limited. However, in addition to the stories, you have the example of their present life. In the assignment you are going to provide "evidence" as to how successfully your subject transitioned through each of Erikson's stages. This evidence will come from direct memories of the time and from an analysis of their functioning as an adult.

The stories from the first three years should be self explanatory. Adult functioning can be looked at as follows:

1. Adult functioning related to Trust vs. Mistrust - Was the subject able to form lasting intimate relationships with people? Did the subject navigate life with friends, family, and other acquaintances?

2. Adult functioning related to Autonomy vs. Shame and Doubt - Did your subject enter adulthood with a sense of autonomy and self-sufficiency? What aspects of their life reflect independent decision making and goal setting?

3. Adult functioning related to Initiative vs. Guilt - Did the individual develop a life of decisive action, or did others largely choose the course? Did your subject adapt to different roles and expectations through changes in their lives?

Criteria for Success

Use the rubric below as a guide to this assignment.

Title Page   10 points

Standard title page with name, date, course, college name and the name of the assignment.

Trust vs. Mistrust   25 points

Relate a story from your subject's past and/or evidence from their adult functioning that defines their success through this stage. Be sure to proclaim a judgement on this...did they, or did they not successfully navigate this stage?

Autonomy vs Shame and Doubt   25 points

Relate a story from your subject's past and/or evidence from their adult functioning that defines their success through this stage. Be sure to proclaim a judgement on this...did they, or did they not successfully navigate this stage?

Initiative vs. Guilt   25 points

Relate a story from your subject's past and/or evidence from their adult functioning that defines their success through this stage. Be sure to proclaim a judgement on this...did they, or did they not successfully navigate this stage?

Mechanics   15 points

Spelling, syntax, and organizational structure of the paper. Clear and organized.

Middle and Late Childhood

5

Attention

The Struggle

So, what does it take to clean a room? What skills does a person need to have in order to clean a room? What cognitive abilities does a child need to have before they can clean a room?

The key to developing the ability to clean a room lays in the development of what Piaget referred to as Concrete Operational Thinking. This develops during middle and late childhood.

When adults clear (organize) a room, we tend to group things together based on characteristics. If you are a fairly organized person you probably organize things like the examples below:

1. Dishes are together in the same cupboard and stacked according to size.

2. Books are upright on a bookshelf and organized by hight (largest to smallest) and maybe even by author or title.

3. Your CD, record, movie, collection is the same thing.

4. If the room in the picture above was yours, each of the bins at the top would be for a specific kind of toy or set of toys. (Cars in one bin, doll clothes in another, etc.)

What are you demonstrating by this is the ability to classify objects along more than one dimension...so, books are not just books, they are also books of different sizes, written by different authors, and with different titles. You are able to see that the book can be described along these multiple dimensions.

This ability is a core aspect of what is developed when a child has Concrete Operational Thinking. Prior to this time, don't be surprised that your child will "clean their room" along one dimension (pushing all their toys under the bed.)

You know this room will not be looking like this for very long when the kids get there!

Learning Outcomes

Upon completion of this Chapter, students should be able to:

1. Describe the characteristics of Concrete Operational Thinking.

2. List personal examples of each of Gardner's Intelligences.

3. Discuss examples of Industry vs. Inferiority from childhood.

4. Discuss potential impact of school closures due to COVID-19 on the development of Industry.

Teaching

Physical Development and Growth

This chapter will cover the age span from approximately age 6 to 11. There is a tremendous amount of physical, cognitive, and emotional development that occurs during these ages. They also enter the larger world through school and the psychosocial challenges of a wider sphere of influence begin.

Physical and Brain Growth

During this age span, children are expected to grow 2-3 inches, and 5-7 pounds per year. They also tend to slim down and gain muscle strength which will enable them to engage in much more vigorous activity.

The **growth spurt**, which begins prior to puberty, begins about two years earlier for girls that it does for boys.

I can so feel for what this guy is going through...sometimes it lasts a lifetime!

Myelination

The continued myelination of the nervous system leads to increased eye-hand coordination and fine motor skills. In the brain itself, there is substantial change in the frontal lobe which leads to improvements in logic, memory, and planning.

Sports and Health

In the Attention section of the Early Childhood chapter we discussed the need to be cautious about involvement in competitive sports. Middle and late childhood are great times to introduce children to sports. Children's participation in sports has been linked to:

1. Higher levels of satisfaction with family and overall quality of life in children.

2. Improved physical and motor development.

3. Better academic performance.

Barriers to Sports

Participation in sports is such a valuable aspect of growth and development it is recommended for every child. However, issues such as poverty, ethnicity, disability, and gender can set up barriers for kids to participate.

Boys are more highly encouraged to engage in sports than girls are and whites are more likely to engage in sports than persons of color (our textbook provides some charts related to these comparisons.)

Despite national statistics supporting the need for physical education, very few schools meet the criteria for 150 minutes a week in elementary school and 225 minutes a week in middle school. Let alone high schools where there is nearly no compulsory physical education.

Here is a great chapter from a book:

Physical Activity, Fitness, and Physical Education: Effects on Academic Performance.

Kohl HW III & Cook H.D. (2013) *Educating the Student Body: Taking Physical Activity and Physical Education to School.* Committee on Physical Activity and Physical Education in the School Environment; Food and Nutrition Board; Institute of Medicine; , editors. Washington (DC): National Academies Press

This, in addition to very poor eating habits, has led to a national problem in childhood obesity.

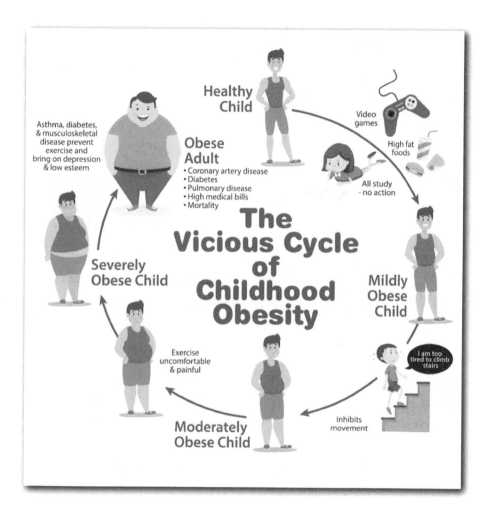

Childhood Obesity

As you can see in this image, the process of becoming obese is gradual and becomes engrained into habits developed early in life.

According to the Center for Disease Control, data from 2015-2016 show that nearly 1 in 5 school aged children and young people (6-19 years old) has obesity.

1. Children with obesity are at higher risk of having other chronic health conditions and diseases that influence physical health. These include asthma, sleep apnea, bone and joint problems, type 2 diabetes, and risk factors for heart disease.

2. Children with obesity are bullied and teased more than their normal weight peers21 and are more likely to suffer from social isolation, depression, and lower self-esteem.

3. In the long term, a child with obesity is more likely to have obesity as an adult. An adult with obesity has a higher risk of developing heart disease, type 2 diabetes, metabolic syndrome, and many types of cancer.

Consider that many children have become "addicted" to their screens and treats. "Dopamine" addictions. What can we do to get our kids off sugar and screens?

Anti-dopamine Parenting

COGNITIVE DEVELOPMENT

SENSORIMOTOR	PREOPERATIONAL	CONCRETE OPERATIONAL	FORMAL OPERATIONAL
BIRTH - 2 YEARS	2 - 7 YEARS	7 - 12 YEARS	12 YEARS ONWARD

Cognitive Development

Genetic Epistemology Model

To explore the cognitive development of middle and late childhood, we return to Jean Piaget. The stage that Piaget identifies with this age is **Concrete Operational Thinking**. Notice that the child now has the ability to have **operations**. Remember that "operations describe the ability to sustain representations of the objects and are able to "manipulate" or think about these objects in their minds."

Concrete Operational thinking entails the ability to sustain and manipulate objects, but these are rooted in the concrete, tangible world. (This is distinct from the NEXT stage which will be **Formal Operational Thinking**, which ushers in the notion of abstract reasoning and the ability to manipulate ideas that have no specific representations in the concrete world.)

According to Piaget, most people did not develop beyond **Concrete Operational Thinking**, not because we are unintelligent but because we so rarely need **Formal Operational Thinking**! Consider all the abilities that your middle and late child attains through the development of **Concrete Operational Thinking**:

1. **Inductive Reasoning** - this is the ability to draw conclusions, assumptions, and generalizations from personal experience.

2. **Classification and Decentration** - unlike the limited pre-operational stage, concrete operational thinkers can categorize objects along multiple dimensions. This allows them to organize ideas and objects better.

3. **Reversibility** - this enables the child to reverse actions, such as pouring water back into the original container or adding/subtracting numbers in their head (which is actually pretty symbolic, but early numbers are learned concretely.)

MOVIE - Anna demonstrates the elimination of
Egocentrism, Decentering, and Reversibility.

4. **Conservation** - recognize that objects do not fundamentally change even if their shape changes. So, these children are not fooled by the water that is poured into the taller/thinner glass.

5. **Seriation** - this is the ability to organize objects along a dimension such as bigger to smaller, or longer to shorter.

Information Processing Model

Another perspective on cognitive growth and development during this time is the information processing perspective. The changes that occur in children in regard to memory, attention, and the use of memory strategies improves as they age and interact with the demands of going to school.

1. Increased capacity of short-term memory.

2. Increased processing speed.

3. The ability to screen out information and focus attention increases.

4. Shifting attention from task to task and transitions in tasks become easier.

5. Memory strategies begin to make sense such as rehearsal, visualizing, organizing, and mnemonics (including rhymes).

6. By age 10, children should have the capacity to use two of these strategies well.

7. Now that memory and recall (rehearsal strategies and organization) are working better, children start to develop a knowledge base.

8. Metacognition is the ability to "think about thinking" or to focus on characteristics of a learning task and decide on a the best strategy to engage the task.

9. Basic levels of critical thinking begin to develop. Children are better at examining solutions to a problem and selecting the best one to utilize.

It is important to recognize that these abilities do not appear in a vacuum. During this stage children head of to school and the activities in school challenge children to develop these skills. This is done by assessing abilities and then engaging **scaffolding** in order to approach a child within the **Zone of Proximal Development** and have them develop new skills.

The interaction between the developing mind and the engaging environment is critical for the development of all these skills.

Language Development and Possible Disorders

Language fluency continues to develop as well. Here are some milestones that occur during this time:

1. At around 5th grade, the child knows about 40,000 words!

2. New and more sophisticated use of words begin to develop (think assimilation and accommodation and the expansion of individual schemas associated with words.)

3. Children begin to lose the typical grammatical mistakes that led Chomsky to develop the Language Acquisition Device concept. They no longer use phases like "I goed to the store."

Communication Disorders

1. Fluency Disorders such as Stuttering impact the rate of speech.

2. Articulation Disorders impact the ability to create speech sounds because of improper placement, timing, pressure, speed, or flow of movement of the tongue, lips, or throat.

3. Voice Disorders represent those troubles with pitch, loudness, and quality of the voice.

Intelligence

As common as the word is, **intelligence** has always evaded a single, simple definition. There are so many different definitions of what intelligence is that it can simply be said that "intelligence is what intelligence tests measure!"

One aspect of intelligence, however, cannot be well disputed. Over the years Psychology has gradually given over to the notion that intelligence is not **just one thing**. There are a number of **multiple intelligences**. We will examine two prominent theories of multiple intelligence here.

Dr. Robert Sternberg

Sternberg's Triarchic Theory of Intelligence

Robert Sternberg identified that there are three kinds of intelligence, tied to the ways in which we apply them:

1. **Analytical (Componential) Intelligence** - academic problems and calculations, much like those measured in a traditional intelligence test.

2. **Creative (Experiential) Intelligence** - the ability to adapt to new situations and create new solutions.

3. **Practical (Contextual) Intelligence** - the ability to demonstrate common sense and/or street smarts (culturally situated - meaning, this one depends on the environment in which someone is asked to demonstrate common sense.)

The Triarchic Theory of Intelligence is not just a descriptive theory, but a prescriptive one as well. Here are some practical applications of the theory.

Triarchic Instruction

Some research has been done on developing teaching methods that include elements of all three types of intelligence. This not only provides a more diverse teaching/learning experience, but capitalizes on specific intelligences that individual students may be more adept at. In the study below, students in an high-school based Introduction to Psychology class performed better when the teaching emphasized their own Triarchic intelligence pattern.

The Effectiveness of Triarchic Teaching and Assessment

Triarchic Principles of Instructional Design

When preparing training materials once can incorporate elements that align with Sternberg's model including:

1. Training of intellectual performance must be socioculturally relevant to the individual

2. A training program should provide links between the training and real-world behavior.

3. A training program should provide explicit instruction in strategies for coping with novel tasks/situations

4. A training program should provide explicitly instruction in both executive and non-executive information processing and interactions between the two.

5. Training programs should actively encourage individuals to manifest their differences in strategies and styles.

Triarchic Theory @ instructionaldesign.org

Howard Gardner's Theory of Multiple Intelligence

The other strong advocate of the multiple intelligence perspective is Howard Gardner.

Gardner has developed a model that identifies nine types of intelligence. Each of us has a degree of intelligence in each of them, but certain types predominate in each of us.

It is tempting to make a couple of mistakes when dealing with Gardner's theory (or with Sternberg's theory). In applications to education, we might liken this to the notion that certain people are good at certain kinds of things and that teaching should be geared toward the types of intelligences they are good at.

MOVIE - Beyond Wit and Grit: Re-thinking the Keys to Success

This might make sense in some ways, but I doubt anyone really wants to go to school to learn things (and in ways) that they are already good at!

Dr. Howard Gardner

Truthfully, the application of multiple intelligence theory is to provide a more broad perspective of the intelligences that people have that make life more interesting. We can then focus our efforts on developing the skills we lack.

What is Gardner doing now?

Howard Gardner is now working hard on furthering his thoughts on intelligence and perseverance (concepts that he terms as "wit and grit.") He recognized that wit and grit are not enough. How we use our wit and grit to do "good works" is the focus of his work. Check out the video below.

Why IQ is Still Important

With all this talk about multiple intelligences, is IQ, or the traditional intelligence testing still important?

In the movie above you might recall Gardner talking about Logic and Language being good as long as you stay in school. This is largely true. The traditional IQ test, developed by Binet and Simon, was created specifically to determine how well people do in school. However, the traditional IQ score (from a number of qualified tests) is only part of the documentation needed today to determine if a person has need for special education services.

IQ scores, however, can have a profound impact on Disability Services and Eligibility for Social Security. A score below 70 on a full spectrum IQ test, along with documentation of functional deficits and challenges, will usually be sufficient documentation for Social Security.

Intelligence across the Lifespan

As with all the concepts discussed in this course, intelligence changes over time! Both theories of multiple intelligences support the notion of change over time. In his book **Frames of Mind** Garner explains that each of the individual intelligences has its own trajectory over time.

Music intelligence, for instance, seems to be the first to develop. Mathematical intelligence also develops early but later than music. Other intelligences develop as we have live experiences (consider interpersonal and intrapersonal intelligences) so these develop later and over time.

Cattell's Theory of Intelligence

In a more general sense, Raymond B. Cattell (creator of the 16 PF Personality Factors) theorized the notion of **Fluid** and **Crystalized** intelligence.

Fluid Intelligence is the capacity to think speedily and reason flexibly to solve new problems without relying on past experiences and accumulated knowledge. This type of intelligence emerges first and peaks in the mid-20s.

Crystalized Intelligence refers to the ability to utilize skills and knowledge acquired via prior learning. Crystalized intelligence rises gradually and remains stable throughout adulthood until it begins to decline after age

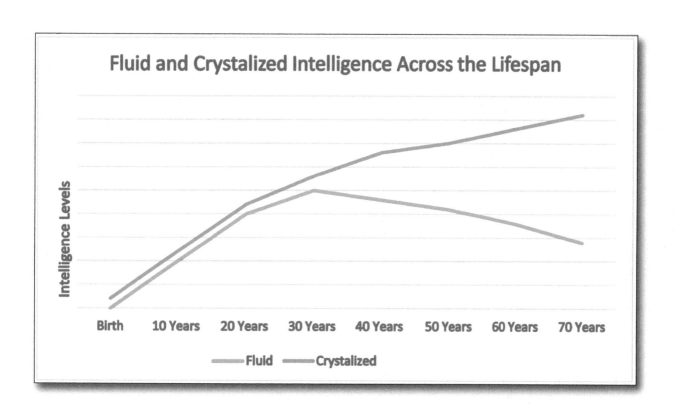

Fluid and Crystalized Intelligence Across the Lifespan

60. Here is a great reference to both fluid and crystalized intelligence on Simple Psychology.

Fluid Intelligence vs Crystalized Intelligence

On the following page is a graphic from this source that shows the change in both Fluid and Crystalized intelligence.

School and Psychosocial Development

Bronfenbrenner's Theory of Ecological Systems

This is a good time to review Bronfenbrenner's Ecological Systems theory as it applies to the increasingly diverse number of social groups a child is engaged in. Bronfenbrenner asserted that over time our social "circle" comes under the influence of more and more distant aspects of our society.

As you can see, the model starts in the middle with the individual.

1. **Microsystem** - made up of social institutions in which the person belongs such as family, school, peers, and religious institutions.

2. **Mesosystem** - this area defines the interactions between the components of our Microsystem. So, family interacts with school, school interacts with peers, health services interact with schools, etc.

3. **Exosystem** - this area includes wider cultural forces such as politics, the economy, mass media, etc.

4. **Macrosystem** - this is the actual culture of the person, and includes all of the social norms, values, and expectations.

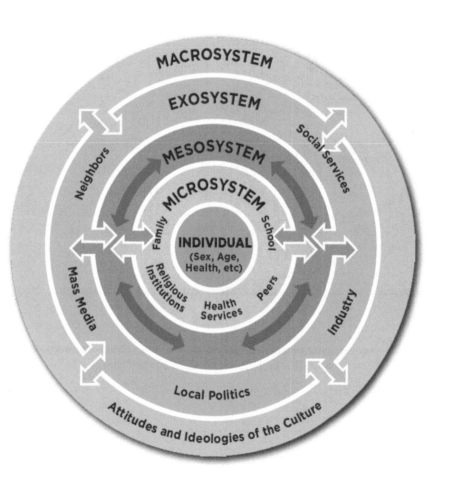

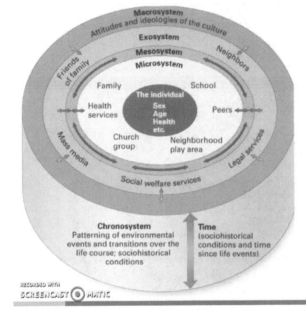

Exosystem

Link between two settings: One is an immediate setting, and the other is one where the person doesn't play an active role.

MOVIE - Brofenbrenner's Ecological Theory

5. **Chronosystem** - this does not appear in our graphic and it relates to how these institutions change over the lifespan of the individual.

As children move into the additional parts of the microsystem and begin to create their identity from these perspectives they also begin to see the wider world and how these systems integrate with one another. The expectations of each of these microsystems are not always aligned.

School

Although many children experience the impact of "school" in early childhood (though child care and preschool experiences), formalized school begins at around age 5 and possibly for the first time, a child's development is keenly being compared to standards. This expectation, realized in in the social structure of "grade levels" in school, shapes a lot of the lives of middle and late childhood.

Early in the history of mandatory education, industrialists realized that school could be used to indoctrinate young people with the skills, knowledge, and cultural expectations they wish workers to have. Public schools began to appear to meet the need for a more educated and literate society largely based on preparing people to work in factories. While some of the basics of "reading, writing, and arithmetic" were explicit aspects of the curriculum, values associated with the role of "employee" or "factory worker" were instilled in the curriculum as well.

Hidden Curriculum

According to Alsubai (2015), "hidden curriculum refers to the unspoken or implicit values, behaviors, procedures, and norms that exist in the education setting. These expectations have larger social meaning in terms of how people "should" behave at work and in the community.

Within the hidden curriculum are positive values such as "hard work" and "persistence", but there are also other aspects of the curriculum that perpetuate inequality in regard to gender, race, etc.

Kindergarten

We hear this word so often we can sometimes lose track of its clearly German roots. Kindergarten structure was initially created in the late 18th century in Bavaria and Strasbourg to serve children whose parents both work outside the home. The term is now used around the world to describe educational institutions and learning spaces serving students from age 1 to 7.

The term "kindergarten", meaning "garden of children" was coined by Frederick Froebel to describe his creation of an experimental social experience for children entering school. The women he trained would spread the notion of kindergarten through the world.

Frederick Froebel

Social Expectations and Curriculum

Keep in mind that the goals of schooling have always been centered on preparing kids to be productive and responsible citizens. Over the years, the details of knowledge, values, and expectations for different ages has changed in terms of technology and modern concepts, but has largely remained the same. The State of Maine maintains policy on the progression of children

Stages of Psychosocial Development

Early Childhood
autonomy vs. shame and doubt

Preschool
initiative vs. guilt

Infancy
trust
vs.
mistrust

School Age
industry
vs.
inferiority

Maturity
ego integrity
vs.
despair

Adolescence
identity
vs.
role confusion

Middle Adulthood
generativity vs. stagnation

Young Adulthood
intimacy vs. isolation

through school (Kindergarten through 12th grade, or K-12).

Maine Department of Education Website

Entering the school environment constitutes a major change in the number of people interacting with most children. It also exposes, sometimes for the first time, the child's experience of being compared to standards of performance based on age.

Industry vs. Inferiority

Note that the "School Age" brings about the psychosocial conflict of "Industry vs. Inferiority." By this Erikson meant that during this time children are interacting with other children and determining, competing, and developing what they are "good at." This "comparison" and "competitive" nature of self-discovery is pervasive within the structure of schools.

Erikson felt that this is a vital stage of development in that consistent praise and encouragement will produce self-confidence and self-efficacy (the perception of being able to do things.) Children can also discover that there are benefits to being industrious and diligent. "Working hard" and the development of persistence in the face of challenges is at the heart of the development that is happening at this stage.

Parenting (Teaching) and...Industry

It is important for all the individuals involved in the child's life to provide encouragement, especially when they are struggling (school work, sports, social interactions, etc.). If children "hear" the message that they are not "good enough" they will believe it!

Parents will need to interact closely with their children's teachers to assure that their children are getting the amount of support and encouragement that they need when they are in school.

A note on schools…

It is important to recognize that schools are social institutions that are largely run by sets of policies and practices that "work" for the majority of students there. They are also often underfunded, understaffed, and certainly under appreciated.

Attacking your child's teacher in response to your child's lackluster performance will not likely create the kind of change you are hoping for. While schools have a responsibility to provide our children with appropriate support and opportunity for success, other resources also need to help facilitate this process. Developing a positive relationship with your children's teachers with an openness to hear their thoughts on what can be done

at home will go a long way in assuring that your children get what they need to be successful.

Failure

Sometimes kids will get a poor grade. Sometimes kids will not score that "easy goal" or may not even make the team. Contending with failure is one of the most important skills for children to learn and the time to do that is now (when the failure is not so devastating… though it may seem like it is!)

- Unconditional Love - we should make it clear the the value of the person is not tied to their performance on any given task. Bringing home poor grades should never threaten the love and care they receive from family.

- Frank discussions about success, failure, winning, and losing are vital. Learning how to lose is as important as learning how to win. In fact, persistence itself, is the very process of continuing to try regardless of repeated failure!

- A winning/successful child is something to be proud of, but parents should be mindful of they ways they may use their child's success to bolster their own status. This can put an incredible amount of pressure on the children to perform. As with all things, balance between intrinsic (personal fulfillment) and extrinsic (parental happiness) is key.

Hannah Learns to Jump Rope

When my daughter was in elementary school she would spend every other weekend with me. I lived at an apartment complex that had a concrete tennis court with no net.

One weekend I picked up Hannah (and her sister Mara) for the weekend and Hannah insisted that she needed to get a jump rope. I obliged and Hannah spent most of the weekend out on the tennis court learning how to jump rope. I went out and taught her some of the elements of jumping, but it was her practicing that made the difference. Unable to jump rope at the beginning of the weekend she was running backwards while skipping at the end of the weekend.

This is NOT an actual picture of Hannah!

The next time she was at my house I asked if she wanted to jump rope again and she said no. When I inquired she told me that on the previous week all of her friends were playing and all of them could jump rope. She had not learned to jump rope and did not feel she could play. She came to my house, learned how to jump rope, demonstrated this at school, and probably never jumped rope again! She simply had to show her **industry** in this task so she would not feel **inferior** compared to her peers!

Moral Development

Lawrence Kohlberg was a psychologist who worked with juveniles. While his work has been criticized for focusing on the moral development of men/boys (his available clientele) it has stood as a model for understanding how our moral thinking changes over time.

The theory is closely tied to Piaget's Genetic Epistemology. Consider that the moral developmental stages that are described in the image above correspond with Piaget's stages:

Pre-operational Thinking = Pre-conventional Morality

Concrete Operational Thinking - Conventional Morality

Formal Operational Thinking = Post-conventional Morality

An Alternative to Kohlberg

Kohlberg claimed that women were morally less sophisticated than men were because they never seemed to score on the post-conventional aspects of his tests. As you can likely guess, this did not go over well.

Carol Gilligan, who worked with Kohlberg, disagreed with her mentor's conclusions. Her own work was summarized in her famous book *In a Different Voice* which outlines an alternative model for moral development based on the different ways in which boys and girls are socialized in making moral decisions.

While Kohlberg's theory can be called the "Justice" perspective, since seeking justice is the prevailing characteristic of the stages, Gilligan's theory can be said to

have the "Care" perspective where relations and communication are paramount in making decisions.

STAGES OF
MORAL DEVELOPMENT

PRINCIPLE

SOCIAL CONTRACT

POST-CONVENTIONAL
(Adulthood)
Moral Reasoning Based on
Personal Ethics

LAW AND ORDER MORALITY

GOOD BOY ATTITUDE

CONVENTIONAL
(8-13 Age)
Moral Reasoning Based on
External Ethics

SELF-INTEREST

AVOIDING PUNISHMENT

PRE-CONVENTIONAL
(3-7 age)
Moral Reasoning Based on
Reward and Punishment

Kohlberg's Moral Stages

Level and Age	Stage	What determines right and wrong?
Preconventional: Up to the Age of 9	Punishment & Obedience	Right and wrong defined by what they get punished for. If you get told off for stealing then obviously stealing is wrong.
	Instrumental - Relativist	Similar, but right and wrong is now determined by what we are rewarded for, and by doing what others want. Any concern for others is motivated by selfishness.
Conventional: Most adolescents and adults	Interpersonal concordance	Being good is whatever pleases others. The child adopts a conformist attitude to morality. Right and wrong are determined by the majority
	Law and order	Being good now means doing your duty to society. To this end we obey laws without question and show a respect for authority. Most adults do not progress past this stage.
Postconventional:1 0 to 15% of the over 20s.	Social contract	Right and wrong now determined by personal values, although these can be over-ridden by democratically agreed laws. When laws infringe our own sense of justice we can choose to ignore them.
	Universal ethical principle	We now live in accordance with deeply held moral principles which are seen as more important than the laws of the land.

Stages of Moral Development vs. Stages of the Ethic of Care

- Kholberg's Stages of Moral Development consist 3 levels and 6 stages
  - **Level 1** - Preconventional Morality
    - Stage 1 – Obedience & Punishment Orientation
    - Stage 2 – Individualism & Exchange
  - **Level 2** – Conventional Morality
    - Stage 3 – Good Interpersonal Relationships
    - Stage 4 – Maintaining the Social Order
  - **Level 3** – Postconventional Morality
    - Stage 5 – Social Contract & Individual Rights
    - Stage 6 – Universal Principles

- Gilligan's Stages of the Ethic of Care consists of 3 stages
  - **Stage 1** - Preconventional
  - **Stage 2** - Conventional
  - **Stage 3** - Postconventional

MOVIE - Kohlberg, Gilligan, and Moral Development

Assessment

Chapter 5 Discussion A

School can have a profound impact on a person's sense of industry (or inferiority). Discuss an example from your own life and the life of your subject related to how school (during this age) impacted your sense of industry.

Chapter 5 Discussion B

Discuss how the impact of COVID-19 on schools may have an influence on the development of Industry.

Chapter 5 Quiz

1. Describe the characteristics of Concrete Operational Thinking.

2. List personal examples of EACH of Gardner's Intelligences.

Adolescence

Attention

Adolescent Storm and Stress Myth

G. STANLEY HALL
BORN FEB. 1, 1846

G.S. Hall, the first President of the American Psychological Association, is famous for describing adolescence as a protracted period of "storm and stress." This statement was published in 1904 and has defined the field's perspective on adolescence ever since. The truth is, however, that just like our feelings about people acting strange in the full moon, the concept of "storm and stress" is largely a myth.

Despite the notion's persistence, an article appeared in the May 1999 edition of *American Psychologist* titled "Adolescent Storm and Stress, Reconsidered."

The article (Arnett, 1999) supports several notions about storm and stress in adolescence.

1. Adolescence is a time of more storm and stress than other periods of life.

2. Not all adolescents go through a period of storm and stress.

3. Individual and cultural differences play a large role in determining the presence or absence of storm and stress.

The article focuses on three aspects of the storm and stress model:

1. Conflict with Parents

2. Mood Disruptions

3. Risk Behavior

The researchers found a large degree of variation among teens in terms of their experience with these aspects. Although the data does support the notion put forth by Hall, it is with wide diversity and is certainly not universal. Despite any storm and stress, "most adolescents take pleasure in many aspects of their lives, are satisfied with most of their relationships most of the time, and are hopeful about the future." (Arnett, 1999, p. 324)

Arnett, J.J. (1999). Adolescent storm and stress, reconsidered. *American Psychologist, 54*(3). 317-326.

Dr. Arnett will come up again in our next chapter as we consider a whole new stage for Erikson's theory!

Learning Outcomes

Upon completion of this Chapter, students should be able to:

1. Utilizing information from functional MRI studies, explain why adolescents may have difficulty with perspective taking using an example.

2. Discuss the impact of current understanding of brain science on perceptions within the juvenile justice system.

3. Discuss personal experiences with Adolescent Egocentrism.

4. Outline aspects of personal identity and their current status in accordance with James Marcia's theory.

Teaching

Puberty

One of the better known aspects of adolescence involves the Biological Clock and the onset of puberty. **Puberty** is a period of time where the person experiences rapid physical growth and sexual maturation. Unlike when we were discussing earlier growth and development, puberty develops in **distal-proximal** direction.

One potentially awkward example of this is that growth the head is proceeded by the development of the nose, ears, and lips.

Gender Differences

Gender differences begin to appear in adolescence. From approximately age 10 to 14, girls will be taller, but not heavier than boys. After that, the boys tend to get taller and heavier. A recognized difference in the adolescence **growth spurt** can be seen in the graphic below.

Sexual Maturation

During this time of physical change, the sex organs and secondary sex characteristics begin to develop. Development of the sex organs prepare the body for sexuality and for reproduction. Secondary sex characteristics appear at the same time but are not necessarily related to reproduction.

For males, these characteristics include broader shoulders and a deeper voice as their larynx grows. Hair becomes more course and darker and hair begins to grow in the pubic area, under arms, and on the face.

For females, these characteristics include the development of breasts, the widening of the hips and pelvis, and the growth of hair in the pubic area and under the arms.

The development of secondary sex characteristics can have a profound impact on a person's development. This is particularly true when we take into consideration instances of late and early development (development of secondary sex characteristics that appear earlier or later than normal.)

Early and Late Development

Of course we recognize that the development of secondary sex characteristics is determined by the Biological Clock. However, "early" and "late" developers exist based on the Social Clock.

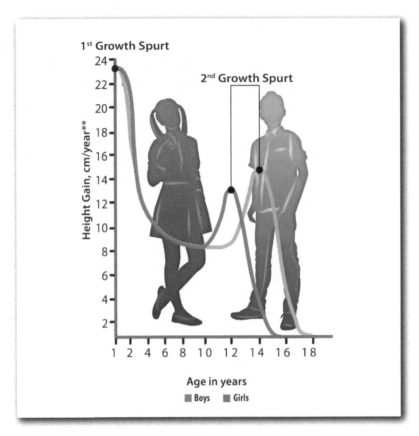

Notice how the graphic identifies TWO growth spurts...one occurs simultaneously between boys and girls (during the first years of life), the second one clearly shows that girls spurt first.

Development	Impact
Early Developing Boys	More positive self image Increased risk
Late Developing Boys	Lower self-esteem
Early Developing Girls	More emotional problems Lower self image Increased risk for delinquency Increased risk for pregnancy and STDs
Late Developing Girls	No significant pattern

As you can see, "violating" the expectations of the social clock can bring about significant changes in a persons development. We might ask why this is so. Why do you think early developing boys may have a more positive self image whereas early developing girls have a lower self image?

Some of our answers will come to light when we talk about the social development of adolescence and the importance of peers and other aspects of our culture on a person's sense of self.

The Adolescent Brain

Just like in the body, there is a significant amount of change and growth that occurs in the brain during adolescence. Based on the latest brain imaging technology, we now know that brain development continues straight through childhood, into adolescence and well into the 20s and 30s.

In the adolescent brain, the focus of this research is in the development that is occurring in the **prefrontal cortex**. This is the part of the brain responsible for logical reasoning, planning, complex cognitive processes, personality, decision making, and social interaction! As this part of the brain is developing, these aspects of a persons life are ALSO developing! Thus we might see some fairly strange behavior coming about during this age. Here is a great TED video.

MOVIE - The Mysterious Workings of the Adolescent Brain

The Limbic System and the Prefrontal Cortex

The limbic system is often referred to as the "reward" center in the brain. It plays a large part in the regulations of emotions. The prefrontal cortex, as we have already learned, has a lot to do with executive functioning and decision making.

These two systems, as interlinked as they are in adults, do not develop at the same time. The connection between the two can sometimes take up to 10 years. During this time the behavior of an adolescent can categorized as risky, emotional, and poorly planned.

Applications in Juvenile Delinquency

Our criminal justice system is based on the assumption that the actors (people) in society are mature decision makers, and those that choose to commit crimes do so with full awareness of the "wrongness" of their actions. But, if adolescent brains are not fully wired to appreciate the "wrongness" of their actions, can they be held culpable (responsible) for their crimes?

Massachusetts General Hospital
Center for Law, Brain, and Behavior

Here are some facts that we know about the adolescent brain:

1. Adolescent brains mature at varied rates.

2. Adolescents have a heightened vulnerability to rewards that drive risky behavior.

3. Trouble modulating impulsive behavior.

4. The better sentencing options for adolescents may not coincide with current law.

I've used this image to describe Freud's ID and SUPER EGO as well. The Limbic System can be seen as selfish and self serving (seeking pleasure - like the ID). The Prefrontal Cortex can be seen as the rational, self-control center (understanding and applying social rules and values - like the SUPER EGO.)

Sleep-Wake Cycles

Another component of the changes occurring in the adolescent brain have to do with sleep-wake cycles.

According to the National Sleep Foundation, adolescents should get 8 to 10 hours of sleep per night. Many get far less than that. While other factors still impact this, one important factor is the changes that occur in adolescent **circadian rhythms**.

Adolescent Sleep Needs and Patterns: Research Report and Resource Guide
National Sleep Foundation

Circadian rhythms are the regular, cyclical processes that occur in your body that govern changes in temperature, blood pressure, wakefulness, and other physiological measures across the 24 hour day. We are all "programmed" to start feeling sleepy at a particular time of day. During adolescence, this timing shifts to a period of time that starts later in the evening and ends later in the morning. That difficulty associated with waking up your teen to go to school is largely circadian in nature! (Of course, staying up all night playing video games does not help either.)

Media and Beauty

As we will see in the next section, adolescents become much more aware of their surroundings. Through the power of communication, television, and social media, adolescents are literally exposed to thousands of images every day that portray what is considered "normal."

Up to age 9 or 10, young girls have very few problems with body image. As they approach the beginnings of adolescence they are targeted with advertising that not only sends the message that imperfection is unacceptable, but that you can actually buy products and/or diet yourself into this perfection.

Body Image: Preteens and Teenagers

Cognitive Development

Upon the onset of adolescence we enter into Piaget's last stage of cognitive development (we will see that other's have expanded on Piaget's theory to describe the cognitive development that occurs during adulthood.)

Concrete Operational Thinking

We learned already that during middle and late childhood, cognitive development builds upon the processes of assimilation and accommodation of schemas that are largely based in the material world. Children of this age are able to maintain and manipulate schemas that they have developed based on their real world experiences.

Formal Operational Thinking

During adolescence, provided there are opportunities to develop these skills, we begin to develop the notion of abstract schemas and with this, the ability to manipulate them. So just as we attained the ability to think

COGNITIVE DEVELOPMENT

SENSORIMOTOR

PREOPERATIONAL

CONCRETE OPERATIONAL

FORMAL OPERATIONAL

BIRTH - 2 YEARS

2 - 7 YEARS

7 - 12 YEARS

12 YEARS ONWARD

about and manipulate concrete schemas in concrete operational thinking, we can now do the same with abstract schemas in formal operational thinking.

Formal operational thinking is largely brought about through education. Day-to-day life is not usually full of opportunities to engage in abstract reasoning, so these skills are not called upon, or in as much demand, as those associated with concrete operational thinking.

Consider this example of some concrete ideas and abstract ideas and how they would relate to homework assignments given in late elementary school and Jr. High/High School.

Example: Let's say that there is a lesson on Communism. In order to have the students demonstrate their understanding of Communism, they assign a written paper.

In Jr. High the instructions for the paper may look like this: "Please write a 3 page paper describing the basic philosophical ideas of Communism."

In High School the instructions for the paper may look like this: "Based on your understanding of Communism, write a 3 page paper describing how life in the US would change if the economy suddenly changed to Communism."

Notice that in the Jr. High instructions the students are asked to simply state the concepts related to Communism. Although Communism is an abstract concept, it has concrete tenants to it and these can be understood by someone with concrete operational thinking.

In the High School instructions, students are asked to speculate on an idea that they could not have encountered directly. Applying their understanding of Communism they would have to imagine a situation that does not exist and speculate on its impact. This is much more clearly an assignment that requires abstract reasoning.

Problem Solving and the Need for Algebra

One of the most salient examples of abstract reasoning is the subject of Algebra. Understand that the ability to understand Algebra necessitates a certain degree of developmental progress along the lines of formal operational thinking. This is sometimes the reason why some individuals may struggle with Algebra...they are developing the abstract reasoning skills as a part of the development of formal operational thinking. Since there are very few common applications for Algebra, these skills can largely undeveloped.

That said...

I am a big fan of teaching Algebra because I believe it develops the key skills needed for effective problem solving. Here is why:

$$-3(x-6)+4(x+1) = 7x-10$$
$$-3x+18+4x+4 = 7x-10$$
$$x+22 = 7x-10$$
$$-7x \quad -22 \quad -7x \quad -22$$
$$-6x \quad = -32$$
$$-6x = -32$$
$$x = \frac{-32}{-6} = \frac{16}{3}$$

1. Consider the equation in the image above. (Some of you might already be breaking into sweats!)

2. The point of Algebra is to consider solving problems that involve "variables" and "variables" can mean just about anything. In this case, we are solving the equation to arrive at a notion of what "x" is.

3. The process of solving an Algebraic equation is similar to Problem Solving. Often, when we are

solving a life problem (not a math problem) we are given SOME information but not all of it, and we have to try and figure out what the UN-KNOWN (x) is based on what we DO know (the information we are given.)

4. Algebra exercises our ability to do this by using an ABSTRACT variable, in this case "x". Solving life's problems (finding the "x") can become easier when we have the ability to use mental skills such as "abstract reasoning", "problem solving", and "symbolic representation", the kinds of skills used in understanding and solving Algebraic equations!

So, while you may be tempted to get a shirt just like this one, you might reconsider. Algebra is like lifting weights...in and of itself it is rarely directly useful, but it prepares you for the problem situations you face in life...you use the SKILLS learned from Algebra every day!

Other Formal Operational Skills

During adolescents we develop the ability to:

1. Understand **abstract principles** that have no physical references (love, freedom, morality, etc.)

2. Describe themselves using these same abstract principles (friendly, kind, understanding, etc.)

3. Engage in **hypothetical deductive reasoning**, which is the ability to think about the possibilities of a situation and evaluate them beforehand. This also means they can start with a general principle (such as civility) and apply it to a number of situations.

4. Engage in **Inductive Reasoning** which is the ability to draw conclusions based on evidence.

5. Engage in **self regulation** both in terms of thinking and emotional control. (Keep in mind that these are developing so they are not yet fully formed as we discussed in the section on brain maturation and juvenile justice.)

6. Engage in **intuitive thought** and **analytical thought**.

Not quite adult...yet

I surmise that nearly everyone reading this book has been an adolescent and has likely had experience with adolescents. It is sometimes hard to believe that all of these adult levels of thinking are emerging during this time...sometimes an adolescent's behavior does not quite match their ability to think. Two factors explain this:

1. We do not always use our highest CAPACITY of cognitive functioning. (We don't always think as high a level as we have the capacity to do.)

2. Adolescent Egocentrism - SEE BELOW!

Adolescent Egocentrism

We have already encountered a degree of cognitive egocentrism when we were talking about pre-operational thinking. Adolescent egocentrism expresses some cognitive development issues, but it more closely resembles what we normally think of when we think of egocentrism, a focus on self.

We will see later that in Erikson's theory the stage of adolescence is about Identity. So it stands to reason that there is naturally a focus on self and the development of the self during this time. David Elkind has developed some notions about the characteristics of adolescent thinking that make it distinct from adult thinking.

Elkind's theory describes a basic sense of **egocentrism** among adolescents, and a number of characteristic aspects of adolescent thinking based upon this egocentrism.

1. **Adolescent Egocentrism** - As discussed, this is a period of time of intense self-reflection and identity development. This aspect of thinking can often come across as selfish and self-centered and can bring about conflict in the family.

2. **Imaginary Audience** - Now, over the years, I have had students struggle with the concept of this being "imaginary." Some contend that others actually are looking at them and judging them. This is probably true. It might be best to look at this as an expression of the **Looking Glass Self** that we have discussed already. People looking at and judging you is one thing, the fact that adolescents tend to be very concerned and impacted by this is what we may mean by imaginary audience.

3. **Personal Fable** - Every generation seems to believe that the challenges they are going through are unique from anyone else. This is particularly strong during adolescence. While the specific circumstances that adolescents are exposed to (drugs, sexuality, etc.) may change over time, other factors like peer pressure, body image, making friends, popularity, etc. are more universal.

4. **Illusion of Invulnerability** - This is probably the most challenging aspect of this stage. Being young, strong, and having so much time in front of them, some adolescents may develop a sense

Adolescent Egocentrism

Adolescents are overly concerned with their own thoughts and feelings

Imaginary Audience

Adolescents believe that others are watching them constantly

Personal Fable

Adolescents believe that their experiences and feelings are unique

Illusion of Invulnerability

Adolescents think that misfortune happens only to others

Elkind's Imaginary Audience:

- Adolescents tendency to feel peers are constantly watching their performance, much like actors are watched

MOVIE - Elkind's Theory of Adolescent Egocentrism

that bad things will not happen to them (they happen to other people.) This can lead to a greater degree of risk taking and other dangerous behaviors (such as unprotected sex.)

David Elkind

Psychosocial Development

Self Concept

As cognitive abilities become more defined and the capacity for abstract thought develops, the self concept of adolescents begins to change accordingly. Asked to describe themselves, the answers from adolescents would include more abstract concepts than would the answers from younger children.

Because identity is a focal point of this age, notions of self concept can be simultaneously defining and in flux. Some aspects of self concept can even be in conflict with one another.

Identity vs Role Confusion

At this point, we have the opportunity to take a look at the next stage in Erikson's Psychosocial Theory of Development. Stage 5: Identity vs. Role Confusion is really the accumulation of notions of self concept developed during the previous 4 stages.

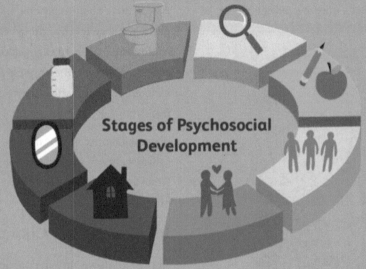

Early Childhood
autonomy vs. shame and doubt

Preschool
initiative vs. guilt

Infancy
trust
vs.
mistrust

School Age
industry
vs.
inferiority

Stages of Psychosocial
Development

Maturity
ego integrity
vs.
despair

Adolescence
identity
vs.
role confusion

Middle Adulthood
generativity vs. stagnation

Young Adulthood
intimacy vs. isolation

Consider the platform of what has already been worked on when a child reaches Stage 5:

1. They have determined that the world is or is not a place that can be trusted and can meet their needs.

2. They have determined the degree to which they can act autonomously from others.

3. They have experimented with taking initiative.

4. They have a pretty good understanding (at least for this age) what they are good at (when compared to others.)

Upon this foundation the child enters into the stage of identity development, which will dominate development from this point on (even though identity is specifically singled out in Stage 5, identity development is at the core of the remaining stages.)

Teens struggle with the question of "Who am I?" and begin to have a sense of the future and the kinds of decisions they will make regarding their appearance, vocational ambitions, intimacy, sexuality, family, interests, and personality. This may be a time of deep experimentation with different aspects of identity as they try different things on.

The Outsize Influence of your Middle-School Friends

Socially, the focus is egocentric and on peers. Peer relationships play a very important role in the lives of teens, sometimes, at least for a while, more important than family. Their **Looking Glass Self** is very focused on peer thoughts and opinions, along with the increasingly complex self-awareness and understanding of the world.

Parenting and...Adolescence

The challenges of parenting children as they begin their journey into adulthood both cognitively and socially, has been documented since antiquity. While our documentation of how life was in the ancient world has always been sketchy, there is some pretty good evidence that adolescence was both very much the same as it is today and very different. In the ancient world...

1. Education was a privilege - in the Greek world, you had to be rich to get an education at all.

2. Fitness was serious business - both as a part of education and the preparation of war, teens were engaged in a lot of competitive physical activities.

3. They were obscene - there is ample evidence that teens would scrawl images of penises and breasts on the walls. Analysis of ancient cave drawings reveal that they were likely done by teens rather than the adults.

4. Teens enjoyed mischief - good food, drinking, and getting in trouble together have been a part of teen life for a very long time.

5. Coming of age was a big deal - today we sense that graduation, getting your license, and moving out of the house are all rites of passage into adulthood. In the ancient world these events were put on by the entire community and usually involved an indoctrination into the roles of family life and adulthood.

6. Marriages were forced - the current process of having the Father of the Bride "give away" the girl has its roots in the ancient agreements that were created between fathers and the husband to be. These were often written contracts between parties, excluding the teen.

7. Teens joined the army - while the girls had to deal with being auctioned off and engaged in marriage contracts, the boys were enlisted in the military.

8. Teens were at risk of being sacrificed - children and teens were often the target of ancient blood sacrifices to the gods.

9. Many teens never got there - due to the high infant mortality rate in the ancient world, many children never made it to the teenage years.

Consider the following quote:

They have exalted notions, because they have not been humbled by life or learned its necessary limitations; moreover, their hopeful disposition makes them thing themselves equal to great things — and that means having exalted notions. They would always rather do noble deeds than useful one: Their lives are regulated more by moral feelings than by reasoning — all their mistakes are in the direction of doing things excessively and vehemently. They overdo everything — they love too much, hate too much, and the same with everything else.

…and this one…

The world is passing through troublous times. The young people of today think of nothing but themselves. They have no reverence for parents or old age. They are impatience of all restraint. They talk as if they knew everything, and what passes for wisdom with us is foolishness with them. As for the girls, they are forward, immodest, and unladylike in speech, behavior, and dress.

We might attribute these to some parents today but they first one is from Aristotle (322 B.C.) and the second is from a sermon presented by Peter the Hermit in 1274 A.D.!

Parents today are NOT alone in wondering how to best manage this stage in their children's lives. Here is some advice from the Mayo Clinic on how to best handle the relationship you have with your teen.

1. Show the Love - throughout the lifespan we are called upon to have unconditional love for our kids. This almost always entails spending time with them, listening to them, and showing respect for how they are feeling.

2. Set Reasonable Expectations - just as when we were dealing with industry, having goals for good grades and scored goals is fine, but focus more on encouraging your child to be kind, considerate, respectful, honest, and generous.

3. Set Rules and Consequences - you want these to be understood and negotiated so these are conversations to have. At the same time, these rules should be constructed in the following manner:

    a. Avoid ultimatums

    b. Be clear and concise

    c. Explain decisions

    d. Be reasonable

    e. Be flexible

4. Prioritize the rules - some rules are more important than others.

5. Set a positive example - probably the most important aspect of this is our own behavior. Kids want to see that we "walk our talk" and that we are willing to live by our own rules.

Puzzle Pieces

I will be going more into my theory of Puzzle Pieces in the next Chapter, but it makes sense to introduce some of it here.

My Puzzle Pieces theory operates on the analogy of a jigsaw puzzle. The picture that all the pieces make is your identity, and each piece is important in the development of the complete picture. Over the course of our lives we construct our puzzle by adopting some pieces that have been created and cut (and are unchangeable) for us, while we actively create some other pieces. All the while, to bring the analogy full circle, we do not have the advantage of the final picture on the box and there really are not a lot of edge pieces!

This stage is a time where we start to collect together some of the pieces that we have built so far from the earlier stages:

1. Trust (am I safe)

2. Autonomy (what can I do)

3. Initiative (are my ideas workable)

4. Industry (what am I good at)

We also start to construct pieces with more intentionality. These can include some initial building of some pieces that we eventually throw away. Some of the pieces that we start to cut include:

1. Gender identity

2. Political identity

3. Vocational identity

4. Ethnic and racial identity

A researcher by the name of James Marcia further developed the notion of the process of identity development that can be applied to **each piece** of your identity. The theory identified 4 different statuses that any piece can be in at any particular time. The status depends on the degree to which the person has explored the options for that piece (crisis) and the degree to which they selected an option (commitment.)

Remember:

1. **Crisis** - means looking at the options.
2. **Commitment** - means selecting an option as part of your identity.

Crisis and Commitment = Achieved Identity (this is me, I looked at the options and selected this one.)

Crisis but no Commitment (yet) - Moratorium (I'm still looking)

No Crisis but Commitment - Foreclosed (this was decided for me)

No Crisis and no Commitment = Diffused (back burner, not currently an issue)

Applications of Identity Status

We can use this theory to look at different aspects of our identity (different pieces) and see where we are at.

We can also track changes in particular pieces over time as we moved them through different statuses. Take this sequence for example:

1. When I was young, my relationship identity was in **diffusion**. I was not actively looking and certainly not committing.

2. Later I began to look for someone to spend my life with and dated several people. My relationship identity was then in **moratorium** since I was in "crisis" (looking at the options), but not committed.

3. I then found the woman who would be the mother of my kids and we started living together. I would say my relationship identity was **achieved**.

4. However, later, we decided to not be together anymore and wanted to pursue other relationships, so I went back into "crisis" and my relationship identity was in **moratorium** again.

5. Interestingly, I then found out she was pregnant. As much as I don't believe these things happen by accident, I did feel compelled to enter back into the relationship, but admittedly I was still in crisis, so my relationship identity was a bit **foreclosed**.

6. We did end up breaking up later (after two kids) and I was back in **moratorium** until I met my wife. She turned out to be the right one and now my relationship identity is **achieved** again.

So, here are the rules:

All aspects of your identity, all the pieces, can only be in ONE status at a given time.

Over time, pieces can move to different statuses.

If something is stuck in an unsatisfying foreclosed or diffused status, you can introduce some crisis, to get things moving!

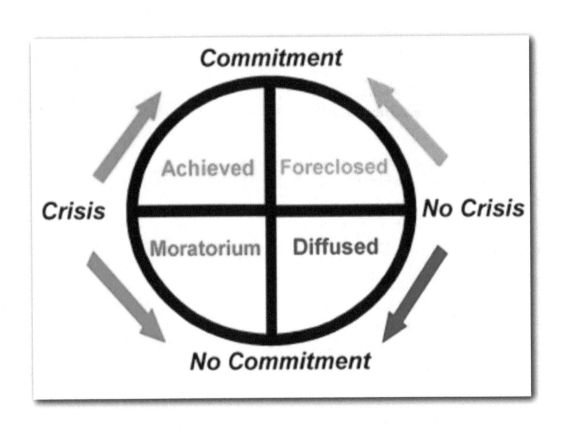

Assessment

Chapter 6 Discussion A

In this Chapter we are exploring the final stages of Piaget's theory. Piaget, however, did not feel that most people ever developed Formal Operational thinking. The fact is, we don't need it "most" of the time.

Discuss times in your life where you felt you were developing or applying Formal Operational thinking and reflect on the advantages this provides for you in those circumstances.

Chapter 6 Discussion B

Consider your own development or the development of people around you. Identify and discuss several examples of Adolescent Egocentrism. Be sure to give enough details in your writing so we understand the exact nature of the example.

Chapter 6 Quiz

1. Consider what we already know about the development of the pre-frontal cortex during adolescence. Based on this work, **use an example** of why an adolescent may have difficulty with perspective taking.

Chapter 6 Assignment

Purpose

The purpose of this assignment is to apply Marcia's they of Identity Status to your current life. When we examiner own development we can sometimes have difficult understanding how we came to be the way we are. In this assignment you will explore the history of some aspect of yourself and map it across the different statuses outlined in Marcia's theory.

Skills and Knowledge

You will demonstrate the following skills and knowledge by completing this assignment:

2. Identifying a single aspect of your current identity that is currently in Achieved Status.

3. Reflect upon the development of that status over time and how it occupied different statuses at different times in your life.

4. Describe the development of this aspect of your identity using Marcia's theory.

5. Upload the paper to the assignment drop box.

Task

For this assignment you are going to select an aspect of your identity that is in the Achieved Status as described by Marcia.

Remember that Marcia's theory states that for an aspect of your identity to be Achieved, you hav to have both been through a "crisis" (looking at the options) and a "commitment" (selecting an option).

Then, tell the story of how this aspect of your identity came to be part of you. In this story identify when it was in Diffusion, Moratorium, Foreclosure, and finally Achieved statuses. Your story may have some cyclical parts to it if you were once Achieved and then a change came along and caused you to look at options again.

It is difficult to discuss this without an example, so I will provide one.

I will discuss my personal identity as a scuba-diver (although this is not currently an achieved aspect of my identity, you will get the idea.)

*Prior to moving to Guam in 1979, I only had dreams of scuba-diving from watching specials on TV. At this point this aspect of my identity was in **diffusion**, I didn't have options to look at and I certainly wasn't selecting any.*

*When we moved to Guam my stepfather stated that he was interested in getting into scuba-diving. My mom said that he would have to include one of the boys and he selected me. Although, I was all into doing this, for a bit it was sort of a **Foreclosure** that I would have to do this.*

*We began to look around for training programs that would allow the both of us to take the class together. This is a sort of **moratorium** process until we found one and joined the class.*

*After the class and the final tests, I was certified as a Junior Scuba-Diver! I had **achieved** this part of my identity.*

*Sadly, we moved away from Guam back to Maine (not the hotspot for recreational diving) I no longer practiced and my diving identity slipped back into **diffusion**.*

There it remains though I would love to get re-certified and dive again, but I'm not actively looking.

Hopefully, you can see with this example how this aspect of my identity changed status through time. This is what I want you to do with this assignment.

Criteria for Success

Use the rubric below as a guide to this assignment.

Title Page   10 points

Standard title page with name, date, course, college name and the name of the assignment.

Identity   25 points

Write a brief paragraph about this particular aspect of your identity.

Story   50 points

Write the story of this part of your identity and include instances of each of the four statuses (Diffusion, Foreclosure, Moratorium, and Achieved.) If you are not able to come up with one for Foreclosure, then describe a situation that would have made this aspect of your identity Foreclosed.

Mechanics   15 points

Spelling, syntax, and organizational structure of the paper. Clear and organized.

Emerging and Early Adulthood

7

Attention

Does Erikson's Theory need another Stage?

Jeffery Jenson Arnett

According to Erikson, Adolescence experiences a primary challenge of identity vs identity diffusion and Early

Adulthood experience the search for intimacy. But is there an in-between stage?

Many of has have encountered individuals, including ourselves, who have taken a longer path towards adulthood. Taking on some of the aspects of full adulthood, but not all of them.

Emerging Adulthood

Dr. Jeffery Jensen Arnett proposed a deeper inspection of the transition between adolescence and adulthood in his 2000 article *Emerging Adulthood: A Theory of Development from Late Teens through the Twenties.*

A New Stage

Some have proposed that we need a new stage of Emerging Adulthood added to Erikson's theory in order to have that theory align with what his happening.

Emerging Adulthood - Incarnation vs Impudence

Incarnation - acceptance of adult roles and responsibilities, with realistic expectations for the future and concrete plans to achieve those goals.

Imprudence - denial of responsibility, concurrent with lack of planning, unrealistic goals, and immodesty.

We will be starting this chapter with a deeper exploration of what is going on through this stage.

Jeffery Jenson Arnett Website

MOVIE - Why 30 is not the new 20

Review this video to see the challenges associated with this
extended delay of entry into adulthood.

Learning Outcomes

Upon completion of this Chapter, students should be able to:

1. Discuss the interaction between temperament and adult personality.

2. Identify and evaluate key culture-specific traits that constitute adulthood.

3. Apply the results of vocational testing to an analysis of personal vocational goals and plans.

4. Identify personal examples that support or challenge the the concepts in Puzzle Pieces.

Teaching

A New Stage?

Early in my education in Psychology, I learned that with advances in understanding of development, the stage of Adulthood was going to be split up into 3 separate areas, Early Adulthood, Middle Adulthood, and Late Adulthood. This sequence of stages has lasted most of my career, but there has always been a hint at the notion that there might be another stage in there!

Of all the animals in the world, humans spend the longest part of their lives dependent on parents to some degree or another. While the definition of when someone enters adulthood (and thus a degree of independence from parents) varies, there is a definitive period of time during which people may have reached the legal age of maturity (18), but have not yet taken on all of the responsibilities of adulthood. Our book formalizes this stage with an introduction to **Emerging Adulthood**.

Emerging Adulthood

Emerging adulthood is defined as the period between ages 18 and 25. The following 5 characteristics of this stage have been identified:

1. **Age of Identity Exploration** - While Erikson identified Adolescence as a time of deep reflection on identity, the 20th century has ushered in a period of "extended adolescence." Much of the processes of experimenting with different selves and choices extends well into the 20s (and even 30s) for some people (we will talk about times when "crisis" forces us to look at choices later in life later in the course.)

2. **Age of Instability** - In part due to the exploration of different aspects of identity, this age tends to change relationships, jobs, and living accommodations more frequently than other stages.

3. **Age of Self Focus** - Keeping in mind the notion of an "extended adolescence", this aspect of identity development continues. However, it does not have the same egocentric quality that appears during adolescence. Emerging adults are found to be very considerate of others, including their parents. They also begin to develop more adult type relationships with their parents, seeing them as "people" not just parents.

4. **Age of Feeling In-between** - During this time, emerging adults may feel that they are neither

adolescents or adults. They feel in-between these. They are typically done with the puberty and high school, they may live outside the home and may be in college, but they may also be financially dependent on their parents.

5. **Age of Possibilities** - The most exciting aspect of this stage of life is the sense that many have of getting on with pursuing their dreams. They have the opportunity to engage in the planning and follow through of plans to be what they want to be. For kids who have grown up in unhealthy homes, this is also an opportunity to escape that environment and build a new life.

When does Adulthood Begin (the Social Clock)?

If you are an adult reading this, when did you first start feeling like you were an adult? Was it a specific event? A specific status you achieved (married, graduated, parent, etc.) Maybe you are an adult in some ways, but not in others?

In the absence of a formal, socially sanctioned, universal event that marks the transition from childhood to adulthood, many individuals gradually acquire more and more of the traits of adulthood, and the exact transition to adulthood is vague.

Cultural Differences

The Social Clock is that aspect of human experience that expresses society's view as to what individuals SHOULD be able to do and be at a particular age. There are social clocks for all sorts of things:

1. When SHOULD a child start walking.

2. When SHOULD a child begin to share.

3. When SHOULD a teen start taking on responsibilities.

4. When SHOULD a person have their first sexual encounter.

There are, however, no universal standards on these. The answers to these questions are embedded in culture.

Different cultures, including the culture in your own family, will have different answers to these questions. To explore this, let's examine your own cultural background.

Adult Job Descriptions

Imagine that you are going to write an ad and try to hire an "adult" in your family. What would you be looking for? What traits would be important for any applicant to have? To help with this, you will need to formulate a job description. Here are some ideas as to what you might include in a job description for an adult:

1. Age requirements.

2. Experience requirements.

3. Specific technical skills - cooking, managing money, mowing the lawn, etc.

4. Specific social skills - emotional control, managing interactions, etc.

5. Specific statuses - has a job, owns a car, etc.

As you can see, it might be pretty easy to come up with a job description for an adult based on the expectations that you have in your own home.

In the Assessment section, I'm going to have you write up a job description and an evaluation form that you can use to determine if the person you "hired" is doing a good job!

MOVIE - When are you actually an Adult?

Personality

Take the Big 5 Personality Test Online

As we age our personalities become more complex and interact considerably with the circumstances we are exposed to. Temperament may be an early indicator of some of the more salient aspects of our personality that remain with us throughout our lives, such as the **Big 5 Traits**.

1. **Openness to Experience** - People who like to learn new things and enjoy new experiences usually score high in openness. Openness includes traits like being insightful and imaginative and having a wide variety of interests.

2. **Conscientiousness** - People that have a high degree of conscientiousness are reliable and prompt. Traits include being organized, methodic, and thorough.

3. **Extroversion** - Extraversion traits include being; energetic, talkative, and assertive (sometime seen as outspoken by Introverts). Extraverts get their energy and drive from others, while introverts are self-driven get their drive from within themselves.

4. **Agreeableness** - As it perhaps sounds, these individuals are warm, friendly, compassionate and cooperative and traits include being kind, affectionate, and sympathetic. In contrast, people with lower levels of agreeableness may be more distant.

5. **Neuroticism** - Neuroticism or Emotional Stability relates to degree of negative emotions. People that score high on neuroticism often experi-

ence emotional instability and negative emotions. Characteristics typically include being moody and tense.

Affirming Personality

As we enter into this stage we are taking on the characteristics of adulthood and engaging in the process of **individuation** which is to say that we are beginning to define our own culture and personalities somewhat independent of our family.

There is a degree of empowerment that can be felt when someone moves out of the house and begins to take on more responsibilities. This is a period of time where some individuals may, if they have not already, separate themselves from some family values and traditions (such as religion or political affiliation), explore personal goals separate from the goals parents have had for them (aligning career options with interests), and express personality and identity traits that are uniquely their own (dress, lifestyle, and sexual orientation.)

Sexual Orientation

Sexual orientation is not to be confused with gender orientation though the two interact with one another. Gender can be said to be a collection of all the characteristics and behaviors that a culture associates with a particular sex. One of these characteristics is sexual orientation.

Sexual orientation refers to the nature of sexual and romantic attraction. For each of is it defines which sex (or sexes) we are sexually and romantically attracted to. Sexual orientation has been a challenging topic in our society due to the mixture of traditional and religious ideologies in this regard.

The terms that capture most sexual orientation include the following:

1. Heterosexual - attracted to individuals of the opposite sex.

2. Homosexual - attracted to individuals of the same sex.

3. Bisexual - attracted to individuals of both sexes.

4. Asexuality - not attracted to either sexes.

Your textbook does cover some additional orientations, but I feel these are more concerned with gender than with sexual orientation. Pansexuality and polysexuality identify individuals who are attracted to a variety of genders and sex types.

At the end of Chapter 4 we explored the earliest experiences of gender identity and gender role orientation.

Language

There are four goals in the study of psychology and behavior:

1. Describe it (language)

2. Explain it (theory)

3. Predict it (models)

4. Control it (intervention)

Over the past few years, the language to describe gender identity has increased dramatically. Just as we learn to better identify other personality characteristics with new words, so are we developing a whole set of terms that individuals can learn to use to identify where they fit into the world.

As you examine the graphic on the next page, take note of how many different ways exist (at this time) for accurately describing the expression of gender in a person. For individuals who are transgender and/or gender nonconforming, these terms have evolved in the language to fill the gaps left by the simple binary representations of boy and girl. Having a more diverse language allows for a more accurate identification of the traits a person has.

While for some this emerging language has been very welcomed and those individuals now have the words that match their inner experience. For others, these new phrases and terms are counter to long-held aspects of their culture. Some individuals strive to understand and accommodate to these changes, others may resist them.

The American Psychological Association is vocal about its position on the issue. Individuals' personal perceptions of gender identity and preferred language should be affirmed and supported.

"Coming Out"

Considering the potential consequences of informing those around you that you have a non-binary gender identity, are gender diverse, and/or have a non-traditional sexual orientation can be a very important and difficult process for some. It is clear that these expressions are not always welcomed in some families and other aspects of our society.

It is not uncommon for some individuals to keep their status secret. Individuals may keep them very secret in fear of rejection from their family, friends, and community. Some who engage in this behavior are said to be "in the closet", the process of revealing, publicly, one's sexual orientation is referred to as "coming out of the closet" or simply, "coming out."

Sometimes the process of "coming out" does not present itself until the individual has moved out of the home and gained a level of independence and support.

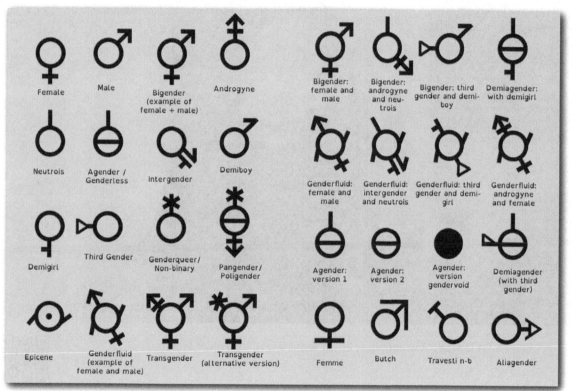

Female

Male

Bigender (example of female + male)

Androgyne

Bigender: female and male

Bigender: androgyne and neutrois

Bigender: third gender and demiboy

Demiagender: with demigirl

Neutrois

Agender / Genderless

Intergender

Demiboy

Genderfluid: female and male

Genderfluid: intergender and neutrois

Genderfluid: third gender and demigirl

Genderfluid: androgyne and female

Demigirl

Third Gender

Genderqueer/ Non-binary

Pangender/ Poligender

Agender: version 1

Agender: version 2

Agender: version gendervoid

Demiagender (with third gender)

Epicene

Genderfluid (example of female and male)

Transgender

Transgender (alternative version)

Femme

Butch

Travesti n-b

Aliagender

MOVIE - The Revolutionary Truth about Kids and Gender Identity

allows adult thinkers to continually evaluate the pros and cons of a situation.

Adult thinkers can conceptualize a "thesis" or perspective on an idea and then construct an "antithesis" or an opposing perspective. This can be done though the creative process or by incorporating multiple perspectives on an issue into the current **schema**. So, as you can see this is truly a process of "accommodation" and "assimilation" continuing into adult level thinking.

Additional Factors

Another aspect of PFO is the consideration of affective factors. In essence, we have the ability to take emotional and personal factors into consideration. This ties in the concept of **Emotional Intelligence** to the concept of adult levels of cognition. Our ability to manage emotional content (the emotions and feelings of others and ourselves) when we are engaged in thinking produces a more inclusive perspective.

Yet another aspect of PFO is a depart from absolute truth to relative truth. By this I mean that individual perspectives have the ability to impact what is "true" to that person. This does not mean that individuals with PFO thinking cannot have strong opinions or consider some concept or another to be "true", but they also have the ability to see things relative to others' perspectives and use this ability to test their own **schemas**.

Career Development

A hallmark of this age is entry into the process of defining one's career. While decisions are sometimes made in Adolescence, the plan (or lack of plan) comes into play in young adulthood. This is also a definitive aspect of our Social Clock, at this age we SHOULD be starting our education or job process in pursuit of our career.

The processes by which we define our career has a very significant impact on our lives. We spend a great deal of time thinking about, preparing for, and engaged in our career. The puzzle pieces associated with career are very important to us. To this end, a number of theories as to how we arrive at "what we do" have been established.

Person-Environment Fit Models

In the early 1900s the prevalent models for career guidance was to seek a match between the environment and personality characteristics of the worker. First we study the individual, then we survey the workplace and match the worker with the workplace.

A good example of this theory is **John Holland's Theory of Career Choice**.

Click here to take a version of the Holland Test

Human Development Models

By the late 1950s, there was a better appreciation of the notion that people changed over time and this concept was applied to how our career changes over time. A good example of this model would be Donald Super's theory. This theory emphasizes the changing roles in our lives and how they relate to our place in the career continuum.

The Life Rainbow graphic on the next page is part of a larger PDF about life stages found HERE.

It is important to recognize that the terms in the graphic "growth, exploration, establishment, maintenance, and decline" relate to our self-concept for work and life roles.

Social Learning Models

Along with other aspects of social learning in the late 1970s, this model builds upon the work of Bandura and the influence our social environment has on our selec-

Realistic

Practical, Scientific, Methodological

Public Health Veterinarian, Public Health Dentist

Investigative

Epidemiologist, Environmental Health Specialist, Health Services Researcher

Observe, Analyze, Evaluate

Conventional

Biostatistician, Data Administrator

Data Driven, Analytical, Detail Oriented

Enterprising

Influence, Persuade, Perform

Public Health Policymaker, Public Health Planner

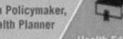

Artistic

Innovative, Intuitive, Creative

Public Health Communications Specialist

Health Educator, Health Promotion Specialist

Enlighten, Inform, Train

Social

tion of careers. Our unique learning experiences over the course of our lifespan are important determinants of our career choices.

Post Modern Models

This 1980s model focuses mostly on actively processing individual constructs related to self in terms of career identity. Individuals set their sites on a specific career and begin to construct an identity around that career choice.

This is a lot like what goes on with interest inventories, career choice assessments, and career/academic planning in traditional settings. While these are perfectly fine and represent very successful strategies, the next model, Happenstance, illuminates some of the reality of chance and how it plays a role in where we actually end up!

Happenstance

In the 1990s, John Krumboltz conducted research that indicated that chance events in one's life has a tremendous impact on career development. Many people he interviewed related that the jobs they were in were discovered not so much through planning but through chance conversations and simply "being in the right place at the right time."

However, one needs to prepare the self for the chance events that come along. Some of the characteristics of those open to chance include:

1. Curiosity to explore learning opportunities.

2. Persistence to deal with obstacles.

3. Flexibility to address a variety of circumstances and events.

4. Optimism to maximize benefits from unplanned events.

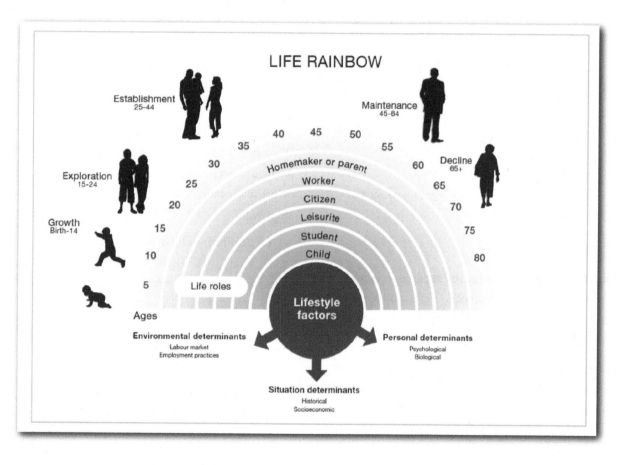

5. The commitment to ongoing learning and skill development.

6. Ongoing self-assessment.

7. Assessment and feedback from others.

8. Effective networking.

9. Achieving work-life balance.

10. Financial planning to incorporate periods of unemployment.

Intimacy

Erikson's theory now turns to the application of one's identity to the tasks of adulthood. Erikson identified that the task of Early Adulthood was the achievement of Intimacy.

We keep in mind that although the word "intimacy" is often associated with "sex", this is not the only application intended by Erikson. His notion of intimacy is inclusive of romantic relationships and sexuality, but it also incorporated deep friendships and connection to community.

Attraction

As we make our way toward my Puzzle Pieces theory, we explore what the book has to say about attraction. What draws us to other people in our lives? How do we go about selecting individuals to be our friends? How do we select individuals to pursue romantic relationships with?

1. **Similarity** - First and foremost, we select individuals who share characteristics with us. In our first social interactions in school, we surrounded ourselves with individuals who shared our same location, age, interests, skills, etc. We connect with others by sharing similar biographies and activities.

2. **Self Disclosure** - As we develop connections with others we establish close friendships with those whom we can share our thoughts without

fear of reprisal, with acceptance, and with little risk. Essentially, just as we entered into the world with the task of "Trust vs Mistrust" so we enter into friendships with this analysis.

3. **Proximity** - Although the availability of social media is presenting challenges to this perspective, we largely choose to be friends with those who are in close physical proximity to us. People who live, work, go to school, go to the same church, the same ball games, etc. in our own communities. Proximity has its impact not because we chance upon these individuals when we move about, but because we come in contact with them on a frequent basis.

Puzzle Pieces

As I venture into expressing this, as yet, incomplete set of ideas, some historical background is needed.

As a social worker and counselor, I had the occasion to work with many individuals, primarily women, who were involved in what could be easily termed "negative relationships." The characteristics of these relationships varied, but they all had some degree of abuse, neglect, and/or indifference by the husband or boyfriend.

I would add that although my experience of this phenomena has been predominantly with women, I do believe that it exists among men. Men, however, are much less likely to seek help in general, let alone seek help with relationships and admit they are being abused. Some rare studies conducted on male victims abuse seem to indicate that it happens far more often than we may expect.

As a behaviorist, I could not understand why individuals would choose to stay in such negative circumstances. I had learned that "punishment" reduced the behaviors the preceded them, so why would being punished (beaten, neglected, abused) bring about a reduction in "staying in the relationship to make it work" behavior? I was baffled.

Relationship Identity or Personality

Admittedly, I found myself in a similar relationship. That relationship revealed to me the first notion of what was to become Puzzle Pieces. My girlfriend was a sweetheart, caring, giving, supportive, compassionate, and affectionate...when others were around. She was not this way when we were alone. It struck me that she had a particular personality that only revealed itself to me. I was equally not mentally healthy and I had a personality that was only revealed to her. We lived out these personalities to each other alone.

After that relationship ended, and remarkably, we mended fences and built a strong friendship, I began to put the parts together to make up the pieces. Considering the lack of motivation my clients displayed to make change and my own experiences with a unique set of personality characteristics that appeared in my own relationships (I was normally a confident, outgoing person, in relationships I became sensitive, insecure, and extremely possessive and jealous.)

Identity Formation

The first concept I included was the notion of identify formation. As we grow up through Erikson's stages we begin to develop a concept of ourselves. In fact, we develop a concept of multiple aspects of our selves. Some of these are complex collections of traits that make our "work self". Others are sets of characteristics that make up our "friend self". Finally, a specific set of characteristics makes up our "romantic relationship self" These characteristics come about through the experiences we have growing up and we incorporate them into our sense of self when it comes to who we are when we are in relationships.

Attachment

As covered in the book, one of the root characteristics of our relationship identity is formulated through our early attachment experiences. Adults who had specific types of attachment end up with consequential types of adult attachment.

1. Secure Attachment as a child - "I find it relatively easy to get close to others and am comfortable depending on them and having them depend on me. I don't often worry about being abandoned or about someone getting too close to me."

2. Insecure Attachment as a child - "I am somewhat uncomfortable being close to others; I find it difficult to trust them completely , difficult to allow myself to depend on them. I am nervous when anyone gets too close, and often, love partners want me to be more intimate than I feel comfortable being."

3. Anxious/Ambivalent Attachment as a child - "I find that others are reluctant to get as close as I would like. I often worry that my partner doesn't really love me or won't stay with me. I want to merge completely with another person, and this sometimes scares people away."

Parental Role Models

Our first models that teach us about relationships and how we are supposed to behave in them come from our parents. At a young age we are exposed to the type of relationship that our parents have and we accept these as the normal ways in which men and women are supposed to interact. I believe that this becomes our baseline for understanding our own role in relationships and without other confounding experiences, we are likely to be very similar to our same-sex parent in our own relationships.

Another way in which parental role models can influence us is when we choose to do the OPPOSITE of what our parents were! If we have had negative role models we might gain from that experience a clear vision as to what NOT to do in intimate relationships!

Happily Ever After

Another early model for relationships occurs in children's stories. I'm not against these stories in any way, but many classic fairy tales not only portray very stringent gender stereotypes (the fair princess needs to be saved by the handsome prince), but they also come to a glorious, happy (every after) ending. One message the sneaks through all of this is that finding a good man, having him sweep you off your feet, and getting married leads to "Happily Ever After."

As adults we know that this is not the way the world really works, but this expectation is embedded into our forming schema of "relationships" long before logic takes a hold. Individuals with strong identities that connect "happiness" with "being in a relationship" will be hypersensitive to ANY threat or imperfection in the relationship. These threats are not only to the couple, but to the persons sense of self.

Television and Media

Early in life we are exposed to television shows (more on this later) and media that both emphasize and trivialize relationships. We are hard pressed to find television shows that do not have a primary "relationship" theme. It seems that it is "all about relationships" and relationships are the most important (and at the same time, least important) aspects of our lives.

This is particularly true in the way in which the media pairs "love" and "sex"...these are practically inseparable in the world of movies and television. Sex is also seen as a solution to relationship problems...who has not seen a television show where an argument ensues, sometimes turning violent, only to be turned into a hot sex scene.

Individuals wedded to this notion will have shallow relationships largely based on physical intimacy. Emotional expression is expressed through sex alone.

Looking at the Next Step

Related to the notion of how relationships and sex are envisioned in the media consider this. Wherever we are in life, we are often living with one foot in the present, and the concerned about what is next. We are a culture of people who plan and prepare for the future. This is a valuable characteristic. If I am in Jr. High I am curious as to what it is like in High School. While I'm in High School, I'm curious about College, etc.

Pre teen children do not necessarily watch television shows that portray the struggles of other pre teens. They are more likely going to look at television shows that show teenagers. The problem with this is, like nearly all of the media, the focus of these shows is often on relationships. A teen is attracted to a girl, a girl and boy are breaking up, etc.

This may have two effects: One, the pre teen gets the notion that being an adolescent is about Intimacy, not Identity. Two, the resolution of these relationships happens readily and quickly in the media...which is not the case in real life. This is a set up for the next influence on the building Relationship Personality.

First Relationships

Even Erikson conceded that despite the focus on identity, romantic relationships begin to happen in adolescence. While this is largely normal it does run some specific risks.

Issue #1 - When adolescent boys and girls of the same age have a relationship, it is well established that the girl is probably much more emotionally and socially mature than the boy. The girl may have very healthy views of the role of relationships, intimacy aside from sexuality, and caring for others. The boy, much less mature, may not be looking for much of that at all. He may be limited to seeking sex and status with his friends. It is easy to tell that makes for some horrible adolescent relationships.

One danger of this type of pairing is that the girl may be convinced that the boy with "love" her if she concedes to have sex with him (he may have even said this.) The fact is, he may say just about anything to get what he wants.

Check out the lyrics to *Paradise by the Dashboard Light*
by Meatloaf

She can then be completely crushed when she realizes that his view of "love" after sex was not the same as hers. If they break up, the boy is relatively less impacted and can simply move on, she may be devastated. If we imagine that up to this time she has been bound to him (much like two puzzle pieces fit together) she will be a mess, similar to what would happen if you pulled those pieces apart!

Issue #2 - Erikson states that Identity is the focal point of adolescence. This is true. Imagine that some individuals begin to formulate a sense of themselves that is deeply rooted in who they are with as opposed to who they are. When relationships are happening while identity is forming, it is not impossible to assume that a person's personal identity can be intertwined and incomplete unless they are in a relationship.

As adults, these individuals may find it intolerable to be alone and may only feel complete when they are in a relationship. This goes a long way to explain my early dilemma about why people stay in negative relationships. They may be abused and neglected but at least they are not alone!

Another possibly outcome of this experience is that the woman who longs for the same attachment that she had as a teen will be attracted to men who are immature, need her to survive, and are often addicted. In fact, the teenager who was just in the relationship to have sex is very similar, in personality, to an addict. In my experiences with clients, it was common for the the partners to also be addicts.

The Pieces of our Personality

In line with Marcia's Identity Status theory, some of the pieces that make up our Relationship Personality were made for us (Foreclosed), others we made ourselves. This constructivist perspective on our developing personality is the core of Puzzle Pieces. Each of these experiences we have help us shape and build the Relationship Personalty and we actively seek compatible partners.

Sadly, if the Relationship Personality is made up of poor attachment, negative parental role models, unrealistic expectations for happiness, a sense of identity tied to being in a relationship, and negative early relationships...these individuals are prone to have the issues that appeared in my clients. Deeply involved and "stuck" in negative relationships or, conversely, going from one intense, deep relationship with one jerk after another!

Sternberg's Triarchic Theory of Love

One of the most balanced psychological definitions of love comes from the work of Robert Sternberg. We were introduced to Sternberg through his Triarchic Theory of Intelligence. Sternberg took the same 3-piece philosophy and attempts to define love in a way that is both descriptive (providing definitions for the important parts) and prescriptive (assisting couples in identifying areas in which they can grow.)

Sternberg describes love as being made up of three components: Intimacy, Commitment, and Passion. A healthy balance of all of these makes for "consummate love."

Relationships that over-emphasize one or two characteristics earn titles such as "romantic love" and "fatuous love." If a relationship is struggling and one or both partners is unhappy, it is useful to review the need to have all three of these aspects of love together.

The Solutions

Hope is not lost! My model is not simply descriptive but it is also prescriptive. There are things that can be done! If you find that you are in this pattern of relationships, here is what you can do:

1. If you are currently in a negative relationship you may have to seek help to decide if you can stay in the relationship while you make the other changes. This may or may not be possible.

2. If you are currently NOT in a relationship - STAY SINGLE! You have to give yourself some time to focus on the following steps without being tied to your usual habits of wrapping your life around your significant other.

3. Engage in activities that will enhance your personal growth and personal development. Hobbies where you will NOT meet potential partners. Activities that you have "always wanted to do." Reading healthy books, attending groups, exercise, etc. These will help change YOU in

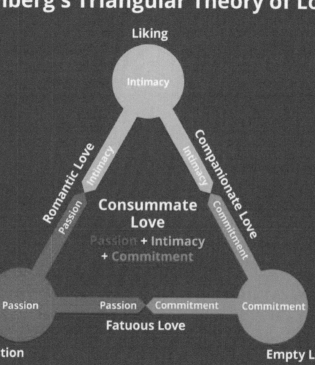

ways that will give you confidence and essentially make you "unattractive" and "not attracted" to your traditional jerk. (If you are in a relationship while you do this, you may gradually "grow apart"...this may or may not bring about negative reactions by your partner, above all, he does not want you to change!)

4. When you feel confident that you will not be tempted to go back into the old routine, you can slowly enter the dating world. You may find that the old type is no longer attractive and they are no longer attracted to you. You may find, instead, that you are attracted to healthier, more nurturing others.

So, here is the "killer" story that drove all this home for me. I met someone who was involved in a series of negative relationships and marriages. She had always ended up in relationships with immature, needy, jobless, alcoholics. When she finally broke free she spent a lot of time with older ladies and went back to school. It was at this point that I met her. She was in the audience at a "singles club" that had invited me to talk about Intimacy from the point of view of Erikson (some of this stuff was under development and I shared it as well.)

She came up to me and described her story as matching what I had talked about. That she had undergone personal growth but that she had to be careful when she was in social situations. She stated that she could walk into a room and almost immediately identify the individuals in the room that were alcoholics. When I asked how she did this, she stated that it was simple...she just identified the ones she was attracted to!

She had figured out that something about her was attracted to this type of person. She made a point of only talking to and engaging with men who she did NOT find attractive. It was through this effort that she found her next relationship. A man who she would have never pictured herself with, but was her perfect match.

Assessment

Chapter 7 Discussion A

To participate in this discussion you will need to complete a few tasks.

1. Complete the Big 5 Personality test on yourself and record your results.

2. Consult with those who have known you has a child (parents, siblings, grandparents) and get a sense of your temperament based on the theory discussed in this chapter.

3. Have your subject complete the Big 5 Personality test and record the results.

4. Have you subject relate any information about their early temperament that they can recall.

With all this information post a report of your findings and discuss the degree to which your evidence supports and connection between early temperament and later development. Feel free to discuss observations of adult behavior beyond the Big 5 if appropriate.

Chapter 7 Discussion B

After reviewing the material in the chapter on Puzzle Pieces, discuss aspects of the model that you feel resonate with you. Provide examples to the degree of self-disclosure that is comfortable and sensitive to others in the course.

You may also challenge aspects of the model. If there are any parts of it that seem to be unrepresentative of your experience, you can discuss that as well.

Chapter 7 Quiz

Prior to taking this quiz you will need to complete the Holland test.

1. Briefly summarize the results from the Holland Test.

Click here to take a version of the Holland Test

2. Provide an analysis as to how the results of the Holland Test align with your current career aspirations. (Be sure to include a detailed description of specific aspects of your future career that meet specific environmental preferences that you have as explicated by the Holland results.)

3. Take a look at your own submission for the Cultural Dimensions of Childbirth assignment. Describe how your Holland results align with the way you approached this assignment!

Chapter 7 Assignment

Purpose

The purpose of this assignment is to look at the cultural based expectations for adult behavior as they are present in your life.

To do this we are going to imagine that we are "hiring" a person to be an "adult". The job title is "adult" and we have to come up with a job description that adequately describes what "adults" do!

Here are some examples:

1. Pay bills on time.

2. Manage their emotions well.

These examples should provide some inspiration for you to come up with a list of abilities, statuses, and activities that you associate with being an ADULT. Based on your own experiences and upbringing (culture) you should be able to identify a list fairly easily.

(Remember, I'm not asking for a job description of an adult job, like an accountant, I'm looking for a job description of actually being an adult!)

Skills and Knowledge

You will demonstrate the following skills and knowledge by completing this assignment:

1. Identify key culture-specific traits that constitute adulthood.

2. Develop a 5-point Likert-Scale based assessment based on these traits.

3. Evaluate your own success in being an "adult" as dictated by your own assessment.

4. Write a title page and paper in a word processor.

5. Upload the paper to the assignment drop box.

Task

There are three parts to this assignment:

Part 1

Write a job description for an adult that includes bullet points for all the characteristics that makes up that job.

Part 2

Write an evaluation form that you can use to evaluate the performance of an adult based on the criteria that you listed in the job description. Each item should be stated simply and then accompanied by a **5-point Likert Scale**. A Likert Scale in this sort of project would be a 5 point scale with the scoring something like this:

1 = Never

2 = Rarely

3 = Some of the time

4 = Most of the time

5 = All of the time

An example of an item on your evaluation form might look like this:

Pays bills on time.   1 2 3 4 5

You can build a table or simply write it out, but make it clear and easy to use.

Part 3

In this part of the assignment you are going to evaluate YOUR adult behavior over the last 30 days. Use the scale that you developed and rate your behavior over the last 30 days and provide yourself with a score. Be sure to include a brief analysis of your results in relation to what a perfect score would look like. Can you explain why your score was not perfect?

Criteria for Success

Use the rubric below as a guide to this assignment.

Title Page   10 points

Standard title page with name, date, course, college name and the name of the assignment.

Job Description   40 points

Job description includes a general paragraph describing the general expectations and then a bullet point list that includes a variety of skills and traits important to possess as an adult.

Job Evaluation   10 points

The job evaluation part should be comprised of the same list of traits (possibly stated in simple terms) that exists in the job description bullets, with an accompanied 5-point Likert Scale on each item. Be sure to include an explanation of the meaning of the Liker Scale scores at the top of your evaluation.

Personal Evaluation   20 points

Recreate the written Job Evaluation and highlight the scores you give yourself in the Likert Scale. After that section, provide a review of your results that includes your total score compared to a perfect score and an explanation as to what factors were involved your attaining a less-than perfect score.

Mechanics   20 points

Spelling, syntax, and organizational structure of the paper. Clear and organized.

Middle Adulthood

8

Attention

Middle Adulthood

I joke every year that the midlife point has been raised by one more year...assuring that I'm still at the halfway point!

Middle adulthood is considered to begin some time in the late 30s or early 40s and extend into the 60s (in some ways, until we retire.) Midlife is by far the LONGEST stage in our development and often represents the stage in which we CREATE our legacy. The stage in which we do the work of our lives.

Of course, many people accomplish great things earlier in life as well. In addition, one transition that can happen is when we transition from doing our work to teaching others. We become experts and begin to prepare the next generation. For many, this is one of the most satisfying times of life.

Learning Outcomes

Upon completion of this Chapter, students should be able to:

1. Discuss examples from experience of expertise and flow.

2. Describe the experience of midlife event (or crisis) experienced by your biography subject.

Teaching

Midlife

Most definitions of "midlife" include an age somewhere between 40 and 65. Arguably it is more about what we are doing during this time than an actual halfway point in the lifespan (a midpoint of 65 would imply a lifespan of 130!)

In this Chapter we are going to explore the longest (surmising this from the span ranging from 40-65) and most productive (this is usually where we get a lot of our goals accomplished) stages in the lifespan. We will start with coverage on the physical changes that occur at this time and lead into how important these are in shaping our perceptions of ourselves.

Physical Changes

Normal Decline

The term "aging" refers to the physiological changes that occur as we move through the lifespan. As our physiological selves peak in midlife, we begin to realize the evidence of our aging in some very defined ways. Multiple factors contribute to how these characteristics change during midlife.

1. Natural selection
2. Tissue damage
3. Decline or loss of cellular function
4. Drop in number of cells
5. Oxidative changes
6. DNA modification
7. Lifestyle (physical exercise, diet, etc.)

Many of these factors are completely out of control, but the quality of life we have from this point on is largely impacted by lifestyle choices. Getting "out of shape" is not an inevitable aspect of aging. These are choices we make in terms of our activity level, choices in food, and our choices related to drugs, alcohol, and stress.

Noticeable areas of aging include changes in the hair, skin, muscle mass (sarcopenia), and lung function. We may also start to notice changes related to our sensory system. These might include changes in:

1. Vision - loss of elasticity in the lens of the eye, floaters, decreased sensitivity to light (difficulty driving at night), and dry eye syndrome.
2. Hearing - hearing problems are more present the older we get.

Abnormal Health Issues

Other changes in our physical condition may result from accumulative lifestyle issues or congenital predispositions for disease. These are not "normal" aspects of aging such as those that are listed above, and they should be treated medically.

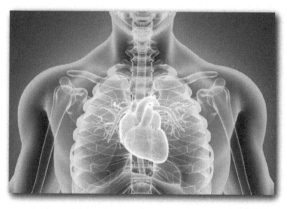

1. Heart disease including heart defects, rhythm problems, and atherosclerosis (the build up of plaque in the arteries.)

2. Hypertension (high blood pressure.)

3. Cancer.

4. Cholesterol issues.

5. Diabetes.

6. Rheumatoid arthritis (inflammation of the joints and connective tissue.)

7. Digestive issues (such as chronic heartburn and gastric reflux.)

8. Sleep problems.

Staying Healthy

As we have already discussed, much of our physical changes are due to genetic mechanisms, but we can act in ways to be the healthiest we can be. These actions include how we attend to our degree of exercise, our eating habits, and our weight.

Exercise

Our activity level and exercise is vital to not only our physical health but our mental health as well. Exercise builds muscle, increases metabolism (for weight control), helps control blood sugar, increases bone density, relieves stress! What is not to like about that! Yet, only about 20% of the population in this age group exercises regularly!

1. Walking or running

2. Weight training

3. Swimming

4. Cycling

5. Stretching

6. Yoga

7. Just about anything!

Adults should engage in about 150 minutes a week of moderate intensity, or 74 minutes of vigorous intensity exercise per week.

Adults should also engage in muscle strengthening activities at least twice a week.

How are you doing with this expectation?

Eating Habits

I started this Chapter by discussing how this stage of life is the one during which we accomplish so many of our life goals. Likely, in part, because of this, we are often busy. Being busy can impact many aspects of a person's lifestyle: increased stress, less time to exercise, etc., but none are likely impacted more than diet. In addition, our culture makes it easy to be busy and "eat" at the same time with the abundance of "fast" and "processed food" choices all around us.

According to the Center for Disease Control, the following represents the obesity rates for different age groups:

Aside from these being astronomical numbers, the highest incidence is in midlife...the busy years!

Modern, processed, and fast-food diets are often imbalanced in terms of nutrition and calories. Typical diets have the following problems:

1. Excess sodium

2. Excess fat

3. Excess sugar

Without resorting to fast-fix diet fads (which work in the short-term but not in the longe term) how can we modify our diet to bring about lasting weight loss and health? Research supports that foods that are high in nutrition and low in calories are the best for us.

Sexuality

Climacteric is the midlife process by which adults experience a decrease in sexual functioning. This impacts both men and women, but women lose their ability to reproduce once they experience this stage.

Women

1. **Pre-menopause** - a transition period during which the ovaries stop releasing eggs and the levels of estrogen and progesterone production decreases.

2. **Menopause** - a 12-month period with no menstruation.

3. Symptoms such as hot flashes, inability to fall asleep, increased susceptibility to stress, are caused mainly by the decrease in estrogen and progesterone production.

4. Physical symptoms that sometimes occur include decreased vaginal lubrication, thinner vaginal walls (decreased sensitivity), and decreased bone density due to osteoporosis.

5. For severe cases, some may engage in **hormone replacement therapy**.

Men

1. Although men retain the ability to reproduce late in life, up to 50% of men aged 40 to 70 suffer from **erectile dysfunction** or **ED**.

2. Causes of ED are primarily linked to medical conditions including diabetes, kidney disease, alcoholism, and atherosclerosis. However, psychological factors, such as stress, depression, and anxiety, account for 10% - 20% of cases.

3. Many of these causes are treatable and ED should not be considered a "normal" aspect of male aging.

Sexuality remains an important part of relationships throughout the lifespan. Being honest and open about these issues with your partner and being willing to explore treatments and/or alternative means of sexual satisfaction may be very important aspects of a healthy relationship.

As we learned about love from the standpoint of Sternberg's Triarchic Theory, couples can put more emphasis on other aspects of their relationship (such as intimacy and commitment) when physical limitations impact the ability for passion.

MOVIE - How Menopause Effects the Brain

Cognitive Development

Changes in Intelligence

Keep in mind that there are so many different ways to measure intelligence. Traditional IQ tests often rely on recalling information and thinking through problems. To a degree, this aspect of intelligence does not change during middle adulthood. This type of intelligence is called **crystalized intelligence** and refers to the accumulated knowledge from experience. It is safe to say that persons in midlife usually have superior crystalized intelligence when compared to their younger peers.

Fluid intelligence represents the ability to learn new ways of solving problems and performing activities. As we enter midlife this aspect of intelligence may diminish. This difference in developmental changes explains why older adults do not show decreased performance in tasks that require experience but may struggle with adapting to new tasks. This lends some legitimacy to

the notion that you can't "teach an old dog new tricks." (Although it is not always the case!)

Cognitive Abilities over Time

One of the most famous studies (ongoing) for how cognitive abilities change over time is the Seattle Longitudinal Study. K. Warner Schaie founded the study and represents one of the leading researchers in post-Piaget cognitive development.

According to the study, middle aged participants perform better on four out of six cognitive tasks than they did when they were young adults:

1. verbal memory

2. spatial skills

3. inductive reasoning (generalizing from particular examples)

4. vocabulary

Numerical computation and perceptual speed seem to decline during middle and late adulthood. Articles summarizing the results of this ongoing study continue to come out. One of the most enduring was in 2006 when Schaie and colleagues published the Seattle Longitudinal Study

The Seattle Longitudinal Study: Relationship Between Personality and Cognition.

Flow

Flow is the mental state of being completely present and fully engaged in a task. When in this state, the individual is able to successfully block out distractions and engage completely in the task at hand. The state of flow is also not concerned with extrinsic rewards, but finds the engaged task to be thoroughly rewarding. The ability to lose oneself in a task and feel attached to something greater combine with other skills and experience to enable middle aged people to engage in flow more easily.

MOVIE - Flow, the Secret to Happiness

Expertise

One of the perks of having years of experience is that you accumulate enough knowledge to be an expert. During this time of life we transition from being the most productive to a position of passing on that knowledge to the next generation. We may do this through new positions of authority in our work or through creative endeavors, or by transitioning to a new career where out experiences are valued even if they are not directly connected to the work that we are doing.

Expertise is characterized by a number of traits:

1. Since experts rely on experience, their actions seem more **intuitive** rather than procedural.

2. Expert processes may seem **automatic**. This is true with even the most complex of procedures. Consider the expert mechanic and how they can quickly and effortlessly rebuild an engine. Consider a public speaker who speaks fluently without a single "umm" to disrupt the flow!

3. Expert thinkers are better at **strategy** than novices. I have seen this in the practice of psychotherapy where a beginner may struggle to find the path toward the solution to a problem, yet the expert counselor will confidently and directly move the dialogue in a productive way.

4. Experts who are continuing to grow in their field are more **flexible**. They enjoy a challenge and like to experiment with new ideas. While this is not ALWAYS true of experts, consider how an expert might approach a situation that purports to be unique...they may say "Show me something that I haven't seen before!" When this does happen, they can become quite engaged and excited about the prospect of new approaches.

Midlife in the Workplace

According to Erikson, as we will review later, this stage is Generativity vs Stagnation. The term "generativity" implies that we are supposed to be "generating" something during this time. This is the period of our productivity, of us creating the legacy that we will leave behind.

During this process we may transition through many developmental stages and efforts to reach generativity and collectively we may refer to this process as our "career" (although it may also include non-work related activities such as raising a family and taking care of a house.)

Work

Work is central to our identity. It is not uncommon for it to be one of the first things we share about ourselves when we meet someone, in fact, we are often asked our name, and then, "What do you do?" The centrality of work in our lives speaks to its role in our efforts to achieve "generativity" and for many it is the primary way in which they do just that.

Job satisfaction tends to peak during middle adulthood. Perhaps we have finally worked our way up to the position we have wanted. Perhaps we have finally made the money we believe we are worth. Perhaps we have even decided to be happy with our work as it is because we have found other aspects of our generativity that are as important (raising kids, community and volunteer work, etc.)

Risks and challenges related to work at this age include:

1. **Glass Ceiling** - the class ceiling describes work situations in which someone encounters an artificial barrier between where they are in the company and where they would like to be. Let's say that a particularly family-owned business only hires family members for the top positions. You may have worked for the position and you can see the position (hence the ceiling made of glass) but you can't reach it, no matter how hard you try.

2. **Burnout** - burnout is the result of a growing sense of loss of control over aspects of your work. Maybe your job description or location is fluctuating a lot, or the results of your work are rarely achieved. The mental health field, along with many helping professions, tend to be "high burnout" types of jobs because the fruits of our labor are rarely directly tangible.

3. **Economic Downturns** - it is not uncommon for organizations that are struggling to survive in economically challenging times to downsize. The most economical employees to let go are the ones making the most money. This puts midlife workers at risk for losing their jobs even though they may have far more expertise than those who are kept on (at a lower cost.)

4. **Overworking** - also a cause of burnout, middle adults in the workplace, possibly threatened by younger and cheaper labor coming in, may spend a lot of time at work. Work without breaks and time for leisure can lead to health problems and burnout. A lot of workers in America do not take time off from work enough. Concerns that keep people going to work without break include:

   - Concern that no one else can do the job.

   - Not being able to afford a vacation.

   - Finding it hard to take time off when you are in the process of moving up in the company.

   - Not wanting to seem replaceable.

Psychosocial Development

Generativity vs Stagnation

According to Erikson, the 7th stage in our lifespan has to do with achieving "generativity." Generativity encompasses procreativity, productivity, and creativity.

Erikson also outlined particular "virtues" associated with each of his stages. The virtue of this stage can be said to be "take care of the persons, the products, and the ideas one has learned to care for."

Characteristics of individuals who are successfully navigating generativity include:

1. Good cultural knowledge.

2. Healthy adaptation to the world.

3. High on conscientiousness, extraversion, agree-ableness, openness to experience, and low neu-roticism.

4. Satisfaction with marriage.

5. Greater global cognitive functioning.

6. Stronger executive functioning.

7. Lower levels of depression.

Midlife Crisis

In 1978, Daniel Levinson published the epic work titled *The Seasons of a Man's Life.*

Levinson proposed that men (consider the publication of this book and it likely applies to women now as well) progressed through a series of developmental stages related to their identity. While similar to Erikson, there are some notable differences and emphasis that Levinson puts on these differences.

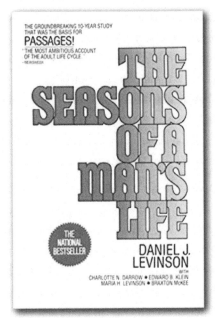

You can find this book for sale on Amazon.

Notice the emphasis on transition points throughout the life. Transitions are noted in early adulthood, at 30, midlife, at 50, and then again in late adulthood. These are times in which we engage in reflection and consid-

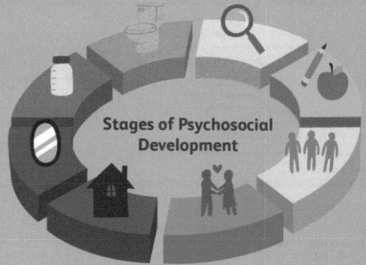

Early Childhood
autonomy vs. shame and doubt

Preschool
initiative vs. guilt

Infancy
trust
vs.
mistrust

School Age
industry
vs.
inferiority

Stages of Psychosocial
Development

Maturity
ego integrity
vs.
despair

Adolescence
identity
vs.
role confusion

Middle Adulthood
generativity vs. stagnation

Young Adulthood
intimacy vs. isolation

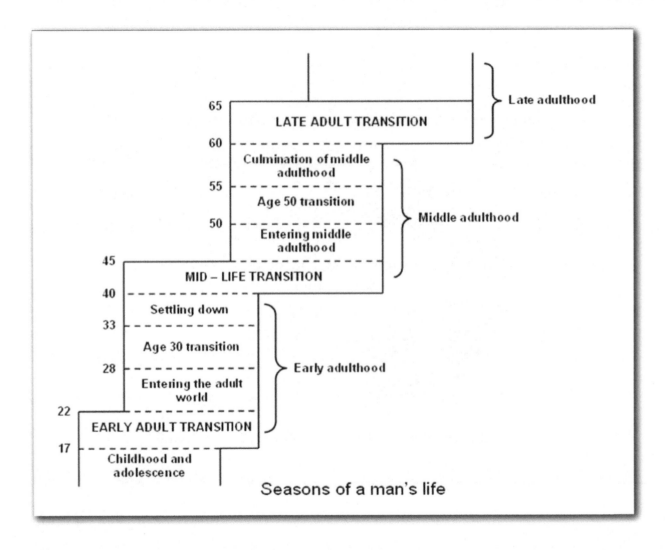

Seasons of a man's life

eration of where we are at and where we are going. During midlife you can see that between age 40 and 45 we engage in a midlife transition and then again, a transition at age 50.

To best understand this process we need to revisit the work of James Marcia and his theory of Identity Status.

Midlife Event and Midlife Crisis

Personally, I have always supported the notion that everyone goes through a midlife event where they introduce, temporarily, a state of crisis (as expressed in Marcia's theory.) This crisis event takes pause and looks at the self, goals set and met, and the current trajectory. There can also be a focus on aspects of the life that are not achieved (ones that are in moratorium, diffused, or foreclosed.)

It may be that we enter into this stage because we begin to notice and feel the reality of aging. Understanding this in a manner unlike before, we may feel a certain urgency to address aspects of our identity that are not yet achieved. So, we may start "exploring the options." Consider the following identity status examples:

1. **Moratorium** - aspects of our identity that we are currently considering but have not yet decided upon are said to be in moratorium. When we enter midlife we may feel an urgency to "poop or get off the pot" as they might say! We need to stop delaying the decision and it is time to move forward.

2. **Diffused** - aspects of our identity that we have not considered nor committed to, but are still important may now come to the front. We my start to consider our future a bit more carefully, we may choose to set aside some goals that we have always had in order to move toward more achievable ones.

3. **Foreclosed** - aspects of our identity that we committed to without a lot of "looking at the

options" may become a focal point of our urgency to change.

Consideration of each of these at midlife should be considered as healthy and normal. However, there is a risk that someone may possess aspects of their identity that they feel insistent on pursing that place their established lives at risk. By this I refer to the concept of the Midlife Crisis.

In this context, I am not referring to Marcia's concept (though that is involved as well) but to the not uncommon event of a person engaging in profound personal changes in order to address aspects of their identity that are in moratorium, diffusion, or foreclosed. Many aspects of a person's life may come under fire and the decisions made may have life-long consequences.

But is Midlife Crisis a Myth?

Why the Midlife Crisis is a Myth

This article really supports that the "popular idea" of midlife crisis is not very real. Rather than a time of double and trouble, it is a time of growth.

MOVIE - Going through a Midlife
Crisis - With JP Sears

Although JP Sears is well known in the YouTube community for his comedy videos, this is a really good video on Midlife Crisis! Check out his other videos too...but you have been warned!

Empty Nest

Once common challenge to development at this age is the changes that occur when the kids grow up and move out of the house.

Empty Nest Syndrome is defined as the experience of great emotional distress after the children have left the home. While some of this is connected to actually missing the kids, it is mostly connected to a lack of alternative roles to acquire once the "role" of parenting is gone.

Parents can also experience a greater degree of marital conflict as a result of Empty Nest Syndrome. Consider the circumstance where a family has centered most activity around the activities of the children. The parents may have been so focused on the children that they neglected to nurture their own relationship in order to enter into this phase. However, data supports that raising children (on average) lowers marital satisfaction and increases conflict in couples. Upon launching the children, parents sometimes feel an increase in marital satisfaction now that the main issues of their conflicts have moved out!

Boomerang Kids

Boomerang kids are those that return home after living independently for a while. Often the reasons for coming back are the same as those for staying at home longer (issues we addressed in Chapter 7).

Although there is research about the negative effects of kids coming back, current data suggests that parents are more tolerant of this. This may be because there is an understanding of how "tough" it can be out there, but it could also be an opportunity to forgo the experience of "empty nest" and to continue to feel that their role as parents are still in effect.

Assessment

Chapter 8 Discussion

Consider the concepts of expertise and flow. Describe distinct situations in which you have experienced a person with expertise and/or flow. Describe any personal experiences you have had where you have expertise and/or have experienced flow.

Discuss the concept of expertise with you subject and provide details on when they felt they achieved it.

Chapter 8 Quiz

1. Interview your biography subject about events in their lives at midlife (they may also discuss other major events) that caused them to take stock of the direction they were going in and evaluate change.

Late Adulthood

9

Attention

Decline?

Although late adulthood is the age of decline, there are many individuals who live lives in direct contradiction to the stereotypes of the elderly that we hold.

In this chapter, we will explore the typical aspects of aging associated with decline, but we will also examine how important attitude, connection with others, subjective health, and the ability to play throughout the lifespan can dramatically impact a person's experience of aging!

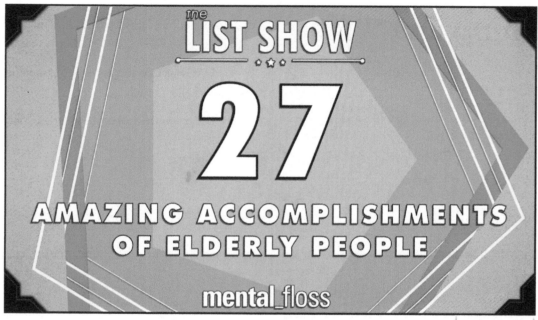

MOVIE - 27 Amazing Accomplishments of
Elderly People

Learning Outcomes

Upon completion of this Chapter, students should be able to:

1. Review personal experiences of memory changes over the lifespan.

2. Reflect on the role of the elderly in our society.

Teaching

The world is getting more gray!

Why gray?

Why do we age? Throughout our lives we replace cells in our bodies with new ones, why don't we keep doing that and live forever?

1. Genetics - it seems that there are certain genes that are responsible for aging and the likelihood of us having a disease. Through the lens of Natural Selection, it is thought that by limiting the lifespan, there is more opportunity for diversity in gene change and mutation in response to environmental changes.

2. Cellular Clock Theory - there are actually two distinct cellular theories, which may combine to determine how we age. According to some research, cells seem to be able to only divide about 40 times. At that point they may simply stop

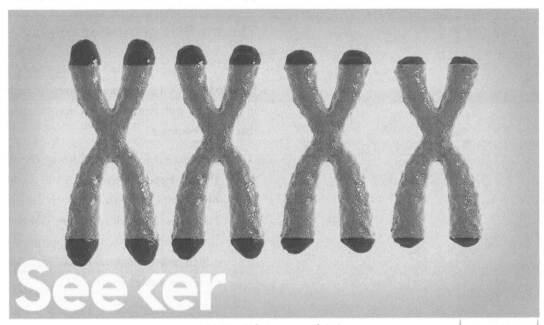

MOVIE - Telomeres and Aging

dividing. Related to this is the science around DNA telomeres.

3. DNA and Mitochondrial Damage - you might remember from Biology class that our cells contain information coded in our DNA and that there is a separate set of DNA in mitochondria. Both of these are subject to damage over time that can cause the cell to lose its ability to convert oxygen into energy using food, and thus they die.

4. Free Radicals - interestingly, when mitochondria produces energy with oxygen they also produce a byproduct of the broken down oxygen called free radicals. Free radicals are unstable molecules that are missing an electron. They tend to take electrons from other molecules and thus damage tissue and cells. While they have the positive impact of destroying bacteria and other harmful organisms in the body, they are also responsible for deteriorating tissue such as skin (wrinkles), eyes (cataracts), nerves (neurodegeneration), vascular tissue (atherosclerosis), and hair follicles (receding hairlines, baldness, and gray hair.)

5. Immune and Hormonal Stress Theories - we have two immune systems in our body, innate and adaptive. The innate system, which includes the skin, mucus membranes and stomach acid, become less responsive to defend the body for all the reasons already mentioned. The adaptive immune system, including the tonsils, spleen, thymus, circulatory system, and lymph system, produce "T-cells" which are programmed lymphocytes that attack invaders such as bacteria and viruses. (T-cells are "programmed" by the introduction of vaccines which equip the body to fight off the specific bacteria or virus in question. We attain this new ability when we are

immunized.) Over time we produce fewer T-cells.

6. Neuroendocrine Theory of Aging (Stress) - stress increases the production of cortisol. Excess cortisol damages the hypothalamus and leads to deteriorating conditions such as diabetes, thyroid problems, osteoporosis, and orthostatic hypotension.

Bodily Changes in Aging

1. Tissues lose the amount of water in them, lose elasticity.

2. Skin loses elasticity and becomes thinner.

3. Sarcopenia is the natural loss of muscle tissue due to aging.

4. All the senses reduce in their acuity (smell, taste, vision, touch, hearing)

Life Expectancy

So, how long do you want to live? 75? 80? 120? Forever?

Developmental Psychologists study aging patterns across the globe. How LONG someone lives is called "Longevity" and is determined by genetic and environmental factors.

The Average Life Expectancy is a statistic that determines the age at which 1/2 of the people born in a particular year will be still alive.

The increases in longevity worldwide are due to genetic and environmental factors:

1. Family with a long history of long-lived individuals

2. Low family history of disease

3. Toxins

4. Lifestyle

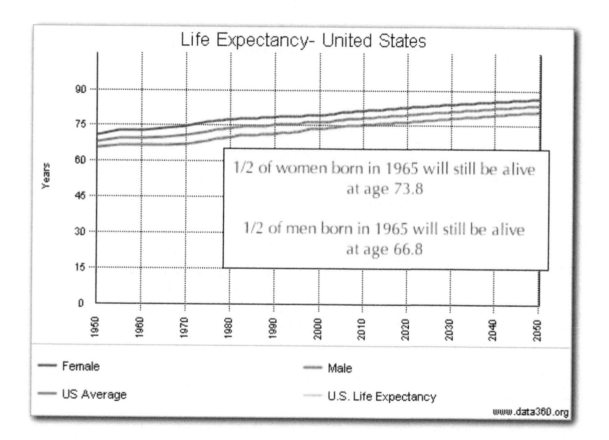

Life Expectancy- United States

1/2 of women born in 1965 will still be alive at age 73.8

1/2 of men born in 1965 will still be alive at age 66.8

Years

Female

Male

US Average

U.S. Life Expectancy

www.data360.org

5. Social class

6. Access to goods and services

7. Access to medical care

Chronic Illness

Because we are living longer, we are more likely to experience one or more chronic illnesses in our lives. In previous generations, the likely cause of death was a sudden onset of an acute illness, such as the flu or tuberculosis. As healthcare got better and more pervasive we have survived these acute illnesses and live long enough to develop the long-term conditions associated with aging.

In addition, the cumulative effect of poor lifestyle choices contributes to the leading causes of death in the world today. Behavioral Medicine is a field of public health that examines and addresses the link between behavior and illness/death.

The differences in life expectancy (women tend to live an average of 5 years longer) between men and women is decreasing since women are more often working outside the home, exposed to the dangers of the workplace, and engaging in the same lifestyle choices as their male counterparts.

Brain Function & Cognitive Processes

What changes in cognitive processing actually do occur as we grow old?

Psychomotor Speed

This is the speed at which we can make a specific response...we might call it "reaction time". People slow down as they get older.

1. May explain other cognitive changes.

2. Decrease in brain white matter which aids in neurological transmission.

Memory

We have all heard the phrase "I'm having an Alzheimer's moment"...but do all old people lose their memory?

To understand the answer to this question, we need to review the different kinds of memory:

1. Episodic Memory---memory of specific events in time (this seems to decline)

2. Semantic Memory---remembering meanings of words and concepts (does not seem to decline)

3. Autobiographical Memory---memory of events during one's life

    1. People remember more vivid memories from their own lives when they were 10-30 years old than when they were older

    2. Less details in the older folks' memories

Concern about memory loss in the elderly has more to do with how that memory loss impacts functioning and anxiety. Having memory aids can help a person function better with memory loss

1. External aids are environmental such as notebooks and calendars.

2. Internal aids rely on mental processes such as imagery.

Fluid and Crystalized Intelligence

It is a good time to revisit Cattell's Theory of Intelligence from Chapter 5. In late life we see the continued reliance of Crystalized Intelligence as the capacity for Fluid Intelligence declines. Unless there is some mental health are disease process, crystalized intelligence should remain stable through the rest of our lives.

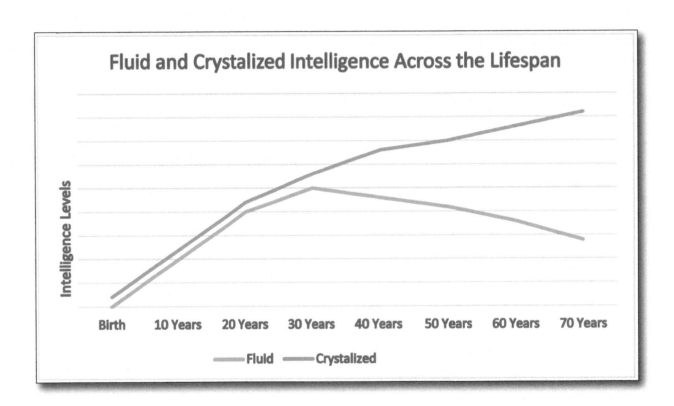

Fluid and Crystalized Intelligence Across the Lifespan

Intelligence Levels

Birth | 10 Years | 20 Years | 30 Years | 40 Years | 50 Years | 60 Years | 70 Years

Fluid — Crystalized

Mental Health

Check out this fantastic resource on all things aging and mental health.

National Coalition on Mental Health and Aging

Depression

A common misconception is that most, if not all, elderly people are depressed. The fact is, among the healthy population, the rate of clinical depression declines over time.

Older people, however, are faced with a number of potentially "depressing" facts...decline in their activity, change in work and societal value, friends and family dying, poverty, illness, disability, impending death...it is not surprising that we ASSUME that to be old is to be depressed!

Dementia and Alzheimer's

Dementia is the term for a class of disorders that impact behavior and cognitive functioning. The most famous of these is Alzheimer's Disease.

Key symptoms of Alzheimer's Disease include the following:

1. gradual decline in memory. learning, attention, and judgment

2. difficulty in communicating (often searching for the right word...)

3. decline in personal hygiene and self-care skills

4. changes in behavior and personality

The definitive diagnosis of Alzheimer's can only be made upon examination of the brain after the person has died.

There are, however, some warning signs.

Warning Signs

Note: This list is for information only and not a substitute for a consultation with a qualified professional.

1. Memory loss that disrupts daily life. One of the most common signs of Alzheimer's, especially in the early stages, is forgetting recently learned information. Others include forgetting important dates or events; asking for the same information over and over; relying on memory aides (e.g., reminder notes or electronic devices) or family members for things they used to handle on their own. What's typical? Sometimes forgetting names or appointments, but remembering them later.

2. Challenges in planning or solving problems. Some people may experience changes in their ability to develop and follow a plan or work with numbers. They may have trouble following a familiar recipe or keeping track of monthly bills. They may have difficulty concentrating and take much longer to do things than they did before. What's typical? Making occasional errors when balancing a checkbook.

3. Difficulty completing familiar tasks at home, at work or at leisure. People with Alzheimer's often find it hard to complete daily tasks. Sometimes, people may have trouble driving to a familiar location, managing a budget at work or remembering the rules of a favorite game. What's typical? Occasionally needing help to use the settings on a microwave or to record a television show.

4. Confusion with time or place. People with Alzheimer's can lose track of dates, seasons and the passage of time. They may have trouble understanding something if it is not happening immediately. Sometimes they may forget where

they are or how they got there. What's typical? Getting confused about the day of the week but figuring it out later.

5. Trouble understanding visual images and spatial relationships. For some people, having vision problems is a sign of Alzheimer's. They may have difficulty reading, judging distance and determining color or contrast. In terms of perception, they may pass a mirror and think someone else is in the room. They may not recognize their own reflection. What's typical? Vision changes related to cataracts.

6. New problems with words in speaking or writing. People with Alzheimer's may have trouble following or joining a conversation. They may stop in the middle of a conversation and have no idea how to continue or they may repeat themselves. They may struggle with vocabulary, have problems finding the right word or call things by the wrong name (e.g., calling a watch a "hand clock"). What's typical? Sometimes having trouble finding the right word.

7. Misplacing things and losing the ability to retrace steps. A person with Alzheimer's disease may put things in unusual places. They may lose things and be unable to go back over their steps to find them again. Sometimes, they may accuse others of stealing. This may occur more frequently over time. What's typical? Misplacing things from time to time, such as a pair of glasses or the remote control.

8. Decreased or poor judgment. People with Alzheimer's may experience changes in judgment or decision making. For example, they may use poor judgment when dealing with money, giving large amounts to telemarketers. They may pay less attention to grooming or keeping them-

selves clean. What's typical? Making a bad decision once in a while.

9. Withdrawal from work or social activities. A person with Alzheimer's may start to remove themselves from hobbies, social activities, work projects or sports. They may have trouble keeping up with a favorite sports team or remembering how to complete a favorite hobby. They may also avoid being social because of the changes they have experienced. What's typical? Sometimes feeling weary of work, family and social obligations.

10. Changes in mood and personality. The mood and personalities of people with Alzheimer's can change. They can become confused, suspicious, depressed, fearful or anxious. They may be easily upset at home, at work, with friends or in places where they are out of their comfort zone. What's typical? Developing very specific ways of doing things and becoming irritable when a routine is disrupted.

If you have questions about any of these warning signs, the Alzheimer's Association recommends consulting a physician. Early diagnosis provides the best opportunities for treatment, support and future planning.

Brain Changes Associated with Dementia

Changes in cognition and memory as we age cannot be separated from the neurological changes that occur during this time.

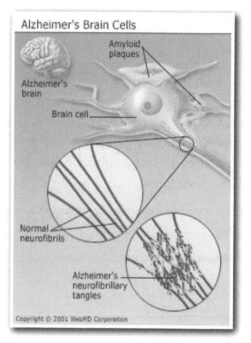

Here are some change that occur on the neurological/ brain level as we age:

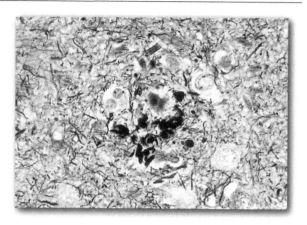

Neuretic Plaques

Neurofibrillary Tangles associated with Alzheimer's

1. Neurofibrillary Tangles---for reasons unknown, fibers that compose the axon sometimes become twisted together to form spiral shaped masses (this is associated with symptoms of Alzheimer's Disease)

2. Neuretic Plaques---damaged and dying neurons sometimes collect around a core of protein

3. Reduced levels of neurotransmitters

The Nun Study

Information about the Nun Study can be found by clicking here. Take time to review the F.A.Q., Videos, and Publications sections of this website.

The Nun Study is a longitudinal study of aging and Alzheimer's disease. It began in 1986 as a pilot study on aging and disability using data collected from the older School Sisters of Notre Dame living in Mankato, Minn. In 1990, the Nun Study was expanded to include older Notre Dames living in the midwestern, eastern, and southern regions of the United States. In 2008 the study returned to the University of Minnesota under the direction of Kelvin O. Lim, M.D. The goal of the Nun Study is to determine the causes and prevention of Alzheimer's disease, other brain diseases, and the mental and physical disability associated with old age.

Psychosocial Development

Integrity vs. Despair

Here we are in Erikson's last stage of the lifespan. In this stage people take on the task of weaving together the threads of their lives and putting them all together into a unified sense of self (integrity) to fail to do so is to have extreme regrets and sorrows of past opportunities and decisions (despair).

People can achieve Integrity and continued Generativity in late life:

1. Volunteers

2. Grand Parents

3. Social Networks

4. Consulting

One of the characteristic tasks to accomplish during this stage is to weave together one's life story into an interconnected "tapestry" of meaning. This "life review" process is common among the elderly as they often enjoy relating stories of their lives and the way things "used to be."

Truth is, one of the reasons this course focuses the Biography assignment on a person aged 65 or older is that it is more likely that a person at this age is ready and willing to tell about their whole lives from this perspective!

Continuity Theory

People tend to cope with daily life in later adulthood by applying familiar strategies based on past experience to maintain and preserve internal and external structures.

In essence, we deal with life using the same strategies we always have!

Change of Identity

Retirement means a change in identity...occupational identity, but this is a very important part of our selves. For many the transition is gradual...some might continue working part time, work another "bridge job", or may not be able to fully retire due to financial need.

For some, retirement is a time to return to generativity...volunteering, projects, helping others, leadership in civic organizations, hobbies, etc.

Work

One of the major transitions we experience is leaving work...remember how important work has been in shaping our identity (whether that work has been in a business or raising a family) our role and status is changing.

Up until the 1930s, when the railroad union promoted a bill to mandate retirement and when Social Security was inaugurated (1935) most people did not think of retiring. (The life expectancy at that time was 65...so it was was presumed that only half of the people who would become eligible to collect Social Security would actually live long enough to get it!)

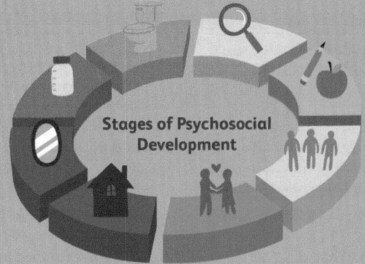

Stages of Psychosocial Development

Early Childhood
autonomy vs. shame and doubt

Preschool
initiative vs. guilt

Infancy
trust
vs.
mistrust

School Age
industry
vs.
inferiority

Maturity
ego integrity
vs.
despair

Adolescence
identity
vs.
role confusion

Middle Adulthood
generativity vs. stagnation

Young Adulthood
intimacy vs. isolation

What about now? Certainly the generation that is about to retire (Baby Boomers) are ready...but does the next generation expect to retire?

Friends and Siblings

Interestingly, through this transition, friends and siblings (rather than children) become increasingly important.

These changes can be a challenge for marriage partners as well.

Personality Changes

New studies on the Big 5 Personality traits are revealing that the largest changes in personality are occurring prior to age 30 and after age 60! Yes, personality changes in late life.

People in this late stage of life tend to decrease in "Openness to Experience", "Conscientiousness", and "Extroversion". Neuroticism seems to increase.

The reason for these changes are varied. Life events such as retirement, widowhood, and losing friends and work may play a role in these changes. People at this age may also be recalibrating their goals and may undergo changes in their personality as result.

Read more about this in the following article:

The Curious Personality Changes of Older Adults

Aging Well

Consider the following list of findings from the Vaillant study at Harvard University:

1. It is not the bad things that happen to us that doom us; it is the good people that happen to us at any age that facilitate enjoyable old age.

2. Healing relationships are facilitated by a capacity for gratitude, for forgiveness, and for taking people inside.

3. A good marriage at age 50 predicted positive aging at 80. But, surprisingly, low cholesterol at 50 did not.

4. Alcohol abuse - unrelated to unhappy childhood - consistently predicted unsuccessful aging, in part because alcoholism damaged future social supports.

5. Learning to play and create after retirement and learning to gain younger friends as we lose older ones adds more to life's enjoyment than retirement income.

6. Objective good physical health was less important to successful aging than was subjective health.

Psychosocial health contrasts the Happy-Well (Integrated) person with the Sad-Sick (Despair) person. One has to consider, however, that there are many ways in which a person can be "sick". This is psychosocial sickness...

1. attitudes

2. depression

3. motivation

4. emotions

5. friends

Consider the six dimensions used to differentiate between the Happy-Well (Integrated) and the Sad-Sick (Despair) person:

1. Absence of objective physical disability

2. Subjective physical health

3. Length of non-disabled life

4. Objective mental health

5. Objective social supports

6. Subjective life satisfaction

Successful Lifespan Development

"A test of successful living, then, becomes learning to live with neither too much desire and adventure nor too much caution and self-care." (Vaillant, p. 61)

As we age we may begin to cope better with our lives and out emotions. Our dysfunctional coping mechanisms may include:

1. Projection

2. Passive aggression

3. Dissociation

4. Acting out

5. Fantasy

More functional tools may include:

1. Sublimation (turning a negative into a positive)

2. Humor

3. Altruism

4. Suppression (often seen as a negative, suppression postpones memories, and even according to Freud, was a "hallmark of maturity")

Summary

So...how do we sum up all of what we have learned about successful aging? I like what Vaillant does in the beginning of Chapter 12 when he refers to old age AA watchwords:

1. Let go and let God

2. First things first

3. Keep it simple

4. Carpe diem

5. Use the telephone

Movie - Secrets of Successful Aging

References

Vaillant, G.E. (2002). Aging Well: Guideposts to a Happier Life. New York: Little, Brown and Company.

Understanding Aging

Growing old fills many people with a sense of dread and fear. Some people don't even like to be around older people. The number of psychologists studying child development is a LOT higher than the number of people studying old age...even though we spend a LOT more time in old age than we do in childhood!

Creative Output

Overall, creative output tends to increase through the 30's, peak in the early 40's, and decline thereafter...though there are ample examples of individuals who are creative late in life.

Wisdom

What does it mean to be wise? Her are four characteristics of wisdom:

1. Wisdom deals with important or difficult matters of life and the human condition.

2. Wisdom is truly "superior" knowledge, judgment, and advice.

3. Wisdom is knowledge with extraordinary scope, depth, and balance that is applicable to specific situations.

4. Wisdom, when used, is well intended and combines mind and virtue.

The Wagon Wheel by Dr. Robert Veon

How do we see Aging? This is what the large wagon wheel reclining against the old birch in the white snow teaches us by its simple beauty. No one of its spokes is more important limn the others, but together they make the circle full and reveal the hub as the core of its strength. The more we look at it, the more we come to realize that we have only one life cycle to live, and that living it is the source of our greatest joy.

The restful accomplishment of the old wheel tells us the story of life. Entering into the world we arc what we a.re given, and for many years thereafter parents and grandparents , brothers and sister,. friends and lovers keep giving to us - some more, some less, some hesitantly, some generously. When we finally stand on our own two feet, speak our own wonts, and express our own unique self in work and love, we realize how much is given to us. But wMlc reaching the height of our cycle, and saying with a sense of confidence, "I really am," we sense that to fulfill our life we now arc called to become parents and grandparents, brothers and sisters, teacher, friends, and lovers ourselves, and to give to others, so that when we leave this world, we cm1 be what we have given.

The wagon wheel reminds us that the pains of growing old are worthwhile. The wheel turns from ground to ground, but not without moving forward. Although we have only one life cycle to live, although it is only a small part of human history which we cover, to do this gracefully and carefully is our greatest vocal.ion. Indeed we go from dust to dust, we move up to go down, grow to die, but the first dust docs not have to be the same as the second, the going down can become the moving on, and death can be made into our final gift.

Aging is the turning of the wheel, the gradual fulfillment of the life cycle in which receiving matures in giving and living makes dying worthwhile. Aging does not need to be hidden or denied, but can be understood, affirmed, and experienced as a process of growth by which the mystery of life is slowly revealed to us.

II is this sense of hope that we want to strengthen. When aging can be experienced as a growing by giving, not only of mind and heart, but of life itself, then it can become a movement towards the hour when we say with the author of the Second

Letter to Timothy:

As for me, my life is already being poured away as a libation, and the time has come for me to be gone. I have fought the good fight to the end, I have run the race to the finish; I have kept the faith. (2 Timothy 4: 6-7)

But still, without the presence of old people we might forget that we are aging. The elderly are our prophets, They remind us that what we see so clearly in them is a process in which we all share. Therefore, words about aging may quite well start with words about the elderly. Their lives are full of warnings but also hopes.

Much has been written about the elderly, about their physical, mental, and spiritual problems, about their need for a good house, good work, and a good friend. Much has been said about the sad situation in which many old folk find themselves, and much has been done to try to change this. There is, however, one real danger with this emphasis on the sufferings of the elderly. We might start thinking that becoming old is the same as becoming a problem, that aging is a sad human fate that nobody can escape and should be avoided all cost, that growing towards the end of the life cycle is a morbid reality that should only be acknowledged when the signs can no longer be denied.

It is not difficult to see that for many people in our world, becoming old is filled with fear and pain. Millions of the elderly are left alone, and the end of their cycle becomes a source or bitterness and despair. There are many reasons for this situation, and we should try to examine them carefully. But underneath all the explanations we can offer, there is the temptation to make aging into the problem of the elderly mid to deny our basic human solidarity in this most human process.

Maybe we have been trying too hard to silence the voices of those who remind us of our own destiny and have become our sharpest critics by their very presence. Thus our first and most important task is to help the elderly become our teachers again and to restore the broken connections among the generations.

The elderly or our "elders" are truly our teachers. They alert us to the dangers or decisions which can affect the process of living toward fulfillment in later years. We are all in "the process of becoming" as Carl Rogers would say. The value or our process will be in direct degree to how much we learn to live. The elders can show us that growing older is not the pathway into darkness but the highway into light and enlightenment.

We want to talk about the elderly and their pilgrimage into aging so that we can appreciate and see them in a new way and they can help us, in turn, see ourselves, as

Assessment

Chapter 9 Discussion

Reflect on the essay regarding Aging by Dr. Veon. What is the message that is in this document? How does this relate to your own feelings about the elderly and about growing old?

Chapter 9 Quiz

1. Based on your experience in your interviews for the biography project, what memory patters (including memory loss) did you note in your conversations? For instance, was it easier for your subject to remember events from their ages 10-30 than later, as is indicated in the notes? Does your subject's memory "problems" interfere with their functioning?

Death and Dying

10

Attention

Humor and Death

Why do we joke so much about death? Does joking make it easier to deal with? Inevitably, all of us will have to face the death of many people we know and love and then ultimately face our own end.

Humor about death can provide us with three things:

1. Relief for our own anxieties about death.

2. Help with coping with the death of others.

3. Ease the stress that often accompanies and surrounds grief.

Learning Outcomes

Upon completion of this Chapter, students should be able to:

1. Discuss cultural traditions of death and dying.

2. Reflect on universal nature of loss.

Teaching

Defining Death

As simple as it might seem to define something like death, it actually somewhat difficult. There are biological, legal, and cultural aspects of the definition of death. According to the Universal Determination of Death Act:

"An individual who has sustained either (1) irreversible cessation of circulatory and respiratory functions, or (2) irreversible cessation of all functions of the entire brain, including the brain stem, is dead. A determination of death must be made in accordance with accepted medical standards."

The fact that we needed to have a "Universal Determination of Death" put into law speaks to the complexity of this issue!

Death is, however, a cultural universal. It is something we will all face indirectly (the death of others) and personality (our own death.) Our culture has a number of different terms that are used to describe death in ways that offset the emotional intensity of death. The notion of death is framed in four different ways in our society: through objects, events, statistics, and euphemistic states of being.

Causes of Death

Something has to come along and finally end our lives. A disease, accidents, wearing out of critical organs, etc. But the leading causes of death have changed over time. Early in human history, disease, accidents and starvation were leading causes of death. In today's world, the leading causes of death are more behavior oriented (the result of poor life choices such as eating, smoking, drinking, acting out, and lack of healthy habits.)

Look at the graphic below which depicts the leading causes of death in the US, the death rate for all causes, and the individual state-to-state death rate.

Developmental Perceptions of Death and Grieving

Deeply connected to our cognitive development, we have different perceptions of death according to our stage of development.

1. **Infancy** - infants do not understand death but they do react to the absence of others.

2. **Early Childhood** - in accordance with Piaget's view on early cognitive development, death, in early childhood may not seem real or permanent.

3. **Middle Childhood** - up to age 9 there may still be some magical thinking related to death.

4. **Late Childhood** - at this stage most children understand that death is permanent and that it will impact everyone, including themselves.

Image or Object	Event	Statistic	State of Being
Flag at half staff	Funeral	Mortality Rates	Time of waiting
Sympathy cards	Family gathering	AIDS patients that die	Nothingness
Tombstones	Memorial service	Murder and suicide rates	Passing on
Monuments	Viewing or wake	Life expectancy tables	Going home

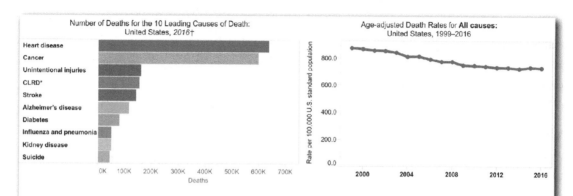

Number of Deaths for the 10 Leading Causes of Death: United States, 2016†

- Heart disease
- Cancer
- Unintentional injuries
- CLRD*
- Stroke
- Alzheimer's disease
- Diabetes
- Influenza and pneumonia
- Kidney disease
- Suicide

0K 100K 200K 300K 400K 500K 600K 700K
Deaths

Age-adjusted Death Rates for **All causes:** United States, 1999–2016

Rate per 100,000 U.S. standard population

800.0
600.0
400.0
200.0
0.0

2000 2004 2008 2012 2016

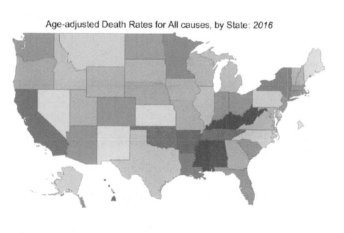

Age-adjusted Death Rates for All causes, by State: 2016

Select Cause of Death
All causes

Select Data Year
2016

U.S. Death Rate for All causes

728.8

Age-adjusted death rate per 100,000 U.S. standard population

Legend for age-adjusted death rate per 100,000 U.S. standard population

572.0   948.9

5. **Adolescence** - adolescences understand death as well as adults, but the personal fable and illusion of invulnerability may impact their perceptions about their own death.

6. **Young Adulthood** - typically not concerned with death and feel there is lots of life in front of them.

7. **Middle Adulthood** - report more fear of death than in either young or late adulthood.

8. **Late Adulthood** - actually experience less fear and anxiety about death.

Elizabeth Kübler-Ross

One of the most famous writers on the process of dying is Elizabeth Kübler-Ross. She proposed that there are stages through which the dying go through. Although there are many valid criticisms of her work, the ideas continue to be useful in understanding the different emotional states that a person can go through when facing any sort of loss.

This same model has been used to guide people through all sorts of transitions and loss including situations at work and in relationships.

Grieving Across the Lifespan

How we deal with loss changes based up on our age (Developmental Perspective.) Here are some lists about how different people at different ages may deal with grief.

How Preschoolers Express Grief

1. Bedwetting
2. Thumb sucking
3. Clinging to adults
4. Exaggerated fears
5. Excessive crying

Kübler-Ross Grief Cycle

Denial
Avoidance
Confusion
Elation
Shock
Fear

Anger
Frustration
Irritation
Anxiety

Depression
Overwhelmed
Helplessness
Hostility
Flight

Bargaining
Struggling to find meaning
Reaching out to others
Telling one's story

Acceptance
Exploring options
New plan in place
Moving on

Information and Communication   Emotional Support   Guidance and Direction

6. Temper tantrums

7. Regression

8. Stubbornness

Helping the Grieving Preschooler

1. Answer the child's question honestly and simply; allow them to talk about the loss; help them share their fears and worries.

2. Provide simple routines.

3. Give the child affection and nurturing; attempt to connect with them.

4. Provide more opportunities for play.

5. Be patient with regressive behaviors such as thumb sucking.

6. Provide opportunities for the expression of painful emotions through play, creative outlets, and talk.

7. Teach them to recognize and name their full range of feelings.

How Elementary School-Age Children Express Grief

1. School and learning problems

2. Preoccupation with the loss and related worries; daydreaming; trouble paying attention

3. Bedwetting; regression; developmental delays

4. Eating and sleeping problems (overeating, refusing to eat, nightmares, sleepiness)

5. Fighting, anger

Helping the Grieving Elementary School-Age Child

1. Keep tasks simple. Explain things before they experience them - new neighborhood, school, church, family routines and changes.

2. Provide a structured environment that is predictable and consistent; limit choices; introduce small, manageable choices over time.

3. Contain acting out behavior; insist that children express their wants, needs, and feelings with words, not by acting out.

4. Encourage them to let you know when they are worried or having a difficult time.

How Pre-Teens and Early Adolescents Express Grief

1. Physical symptoms (headaches, stomachaches, sleeping and eating disorders, hypochondria) Wide mood swings

2. Able to verbally expresses emotions

3. Feelings of helplessness and hopelessness

4. Increase in risk-taking and self-destructive behaviors

5. Anger; aggression; fighting; oppositional behavior

6. Withdrawal from adults

7. Depression; sadness

8. Lack of concentration and attention

9. Identity confusion; testing limits

Helping the Grieving Pre-Teen and Early Adolescent

1. Accept that they will experience mood swings and physical symptoms.

2. Encourage them to honestly recognize their painful feelings and find positive outlets in physical and creative activities.

3. Listen for the feelings behind their words and actions and respond with empathy.

4. Be truthful and factual in explaining the loss.

5. Help them develop and maintain their sense of identity.

6. Allow preteens to make choices that are not harmful.

7. Encourage safe expressions and experiences of beginning independence.

Healthcare and Dying

Curative Care is the delivery of medical services with the intent on overcoming disease and/or illness. **Palliative Care** is the delivery of medical services to provide comfort and relief from physical and emotional pain to patients throughout their illness. There comes a point in the disease or illness process that people may choose to only receive palliative care without any curative care. Services that have evolved around this approach have come to be known as **Hospice Care**.

Hospice

Hospice involves a team of medical care providers, volunteers, and other important people to provide terminally ill patients with medical, psychological, and spiritual support through the dying process. Hospice services also focus on family and caregivers through this process.

Maine Hospice Council

The **Maine Hospice Council** is the central advocacy, policy development, and educational center for palliative and hospice care in Maine. Initiatives within this organization include:

1. Hospice/Veteran Partnership

2. Maine Physician Orders for Life Sustaining Treatment Coalition (a project to create ways to enforce patient choice in the use of life-sustaining efforts.)

3. The Maine Pain Initiative

4. Hospice and Corrections

5. ALS Maine Collaborative

Advanced Directives

According to Maine Health

"Under Maine law, the term "advance directive" means any spoken or written instructions you give about the health care you want if a time comes when you are too ill to decide. Should you become too ill to make choices about your care, an advance directive will let others know which treatments/interventions you want and which you do not.

"A health care Advance Directive can give you and your family peace of mind. Documenting your health care wishes spares loved ones the burden of making tough end of life decisions.

"Advance directives allow for many choices. By completing an advance directive, you can identify treatments you want/don't want, state your wishes about donating your body, organs and/or tissues at death, outline your wishes about burial and funeral arrangements, and even state your wishes about resuscitation."

Access copies of Advanced Directives from the Maine Hospital Association

Human Development and Dying

While the process dying is certainly a major transition in life for the person who experiences it, it is also a transition for other family members and caregivers. Throughout this course we have been talking about identity, and identity is closely timed to others in our lives. When people get sick and die our identity in relation to those individuals change.

Caregivers

Many people understand the role of parents caring for their children, but when the parent ages, there may be time where the roles reverse, and the children become the caregivers for their parents. The same applies to spouses and partners who may transition from a partnership role into a caregiving role.

Even though many people may embrace these new roles with each other, any transition in role can create strain.

As a social worker in home care, a principle focus of my work was to ensure that caregivers provided the support and care they needed to continue the very important work that they are doing. With support and shared responsibilities, family members can work together to transition through the process of dying very successfully.

However, there are times where the strain of the changed role can become too much to bear. Reluctant to have the patient placed in a facility, caregivers can become quite fragile and sick themselves. Sometimes this process can lead to problems such as abuse and neglect of the patient.

Loss of Children

There is probably no greater sense of loss than that of a parent losing a child. Parents may experience intense grief that may last for years and perhaps the rest of their lives. Trauma will sometimes create a sense of the world being "wrong" and "unsafe", and the death of a child can create this sense of trauma.

Loss of Parents

At one point in our life, we have to face the loss of our own parents. While this is an expected transition among children who are adults, it can happen when children are young as well.

The loss of a parent while still a child is associated with some adjustment problems including:

1. Persistent difficulty in talking about the dead person.
2. Persistent or destructive aggressive behavior.
3. Persistent anxiety, clinging, or fears.
4. Somatic complaints (stomachaches, headaches, etc.)
5. Eating disturbance.
6. Marked social withdrawal.
7. School difficulties or serious academic reversal.
8. Persistent self-blame or guilt
9. Self-destructive behaviors.

The Maine Center for Grieving Children *was founded in 1987 and provides support and resources to grieving children.*

Of course, this can all be happening in the context of an entire family dealing with the death of the parent. When talking to children about death, it is important to use real words and be straight forward about what is happening and involve them in the processes.

Rituals, Rites and Religion

Tasks of Mourning

When experiencing a loss there are four tasks that the mourner needs to accomplish:

1. Acceptance that the loss has occurred.

2. Working through the pain and grief.

3. Adjusting to life without the deceased.

4. Starting a new life while still maintaining a connection with the deceased.

Support groups, religious practices, community connection, and family/friends are key to helping with these transitions.

Cultural Aspects of Dying

Dying is, of course, a cultural universal, and all cultures have developed rituals, rites, and processes to deal with it. In Western culture we may be familiar with such rituals as funerals and wakes associated with death. Some of these are deeply tied to religious traditions.

When someone Dies

When a person dies, there are cultural processes by which we inform members of the community. These happen with civic organizations, churches, and most commonly, through the obituary pages and resources in the newspapers and on the web.

Obituaries are brief descriptions of the person's life that provide the reader with a glimpse of the individual, who they were and their surviving family members. People who are in the process of dying often write their own obituary, or it falls to a member of the family.

Central Maine Obituaries

Visit this page to read some obituaries

Funerals

Funerals are organized gatherings of individuals associated with the person who has died. These can occur at a funeral home, in a religious center, or even at the grave site (or just about anywhere.)

The ritual is to have people gather to share their sense of loss and provide communal support to the family and friends of the person who passed away. This is sometimes associated with a **wake** or a **viewing** where people can come and spend time in the presence of the body (or ashes) of the person who has died.

Burials and Cremation

In many cultures the body of the person who has died is prepared in some ritualistic way. Icons such as coffins and urns (for the the ashes of someone who has been cremated) are symbols of death in our culture. **Cemeteries** are areas of land where individual bodies are buried or placed in a **crypt**. These rituals are pragmatic as much as they are sacred and part of the cultural process of mourning.

After a person dies, their body begins to decompose. The preparations that go into burials and cremations provide for a way to deal with the decomposing body in a safe, honorable, and healthy way.

Religious Rites and Practices

Information on the practices related to death for a number of religions can be found at https://religion-mediacentre.org.uk

This site contains detailed information about the rituals associated with:

1. Buddhism
2. Christianity
3. Islam
4. Hinduism
5. Judaism
6. Sikhi

MOVIE - Behind the Scenes at a Funeral Home

But...what if we could live a whole lot longer?

Scientists Extend Lifespan of these
Animals by 500%

Assessment

Chapter 10 Discussion

Consider the experiences you have had with death and dying. Share stories about the events, rituals, and experiences you have had. Relate how these may or may not have been important in your own process of dealing with the death.

Chapter 10 Assignment

Loss

Throughout our lives we experience joys associated with people, places, possessions, and passions. As all things do, these things come to an end and we experience loss.

Loss can be a simple matter of losing a cherished picture of from our prom night, or it can be dark and threatening such as our personal death or the death of someone close to us.

Feelings of loss are universal to the human experience and along with accounting for the lowest of miseries, remind us of the most uplifting happiness.

In Mark Twain's (1835–1910) Autobiography, edited by Charles Neider (1959), Twain writes of the death of his daughter Susie Clemens of meningitis on August 18, 1896. He explains how "a man, all unprepared, can receive a thunder-stroke like that and live. . . . It will take mind and memory months and possibly years to gather together the details and thus learn and know the whole extent of the loss."

He further goes on to write of his personal loss, by using the metaphor of losing one's home. "A man's house burns down. The smoking wreckage represents only a ruined home that was dear through years of use and pleasant associations. By and by, as the days and weeks go on, first he misses this, then that, then the other thing. And when he casts about for it he finds that it was in that house. Always it is an essential— there was but one of its kind. It cannot be replaced. It was in that house. It is irrevocably lost. . . . It will be years before the tale of lost essentials is complete, and not till then can he truly know the magnitude of his disaster."

Purpose

The purpose of this assignment is for you to encounter the universal quality of the concept of loss. This will involve another period of time with your subject in the biography.

You will be exploring the similarities between the experience of loss that your subject recollects, and a personal experience of loss. The loss does not have to be the same kind, yet it will have similar attributes to it. Their loss may be of a dear friend and you may have lost your house in a fire...still they are very similar in some ways.

Your task is to outline how they are similar.

Skills and Knowledge

Completing this assignments will enable you to:

1. Research universal aspects of loss.

2. Outline two stories of loss.

3. Summarize the similarities based on your research on the universal aspects of loss.

4. Write a title page and paper in a word processor.

5. Upload the paper to the assignment drop box.

Task

You will engage in the following steps:

1. Research in our text and other sources (including online sources) the universal qualities of the experience of loss.

2. Meet with your subject and ask them to describe a time at which they experienced a loss. It can be any type of experience they want to talk about. Be sure to not allow them to feel that they need to share stories they do not wish to share.

3. Reflect on a loss that you have had. It could be the same kind of loss or a totally different one.

4. Write out each of these stories with particular attention to the details that hint and the universal experience of loss.

5. Write a brief essay as to the similarities between the two losses/

Criteria for Success

Use the rubric below as a guide to this assignment.

Title Page   5 points

Standard title page with name, date, course, college name and the name of the assignment.

Research   20 points

Outline what you have found out about the universal experience of loss.

Story #1   20 points

Write out the story, in detail, of the loss experienced by your subject.

Story #2   20 points

Write out the story, in detail, of the loss experienced by you.

Essay   20 points

Briefly discuss the similarities between the two loss experiences based on your research.

Mechanics   10 points

Spelling, syntax, and organizational structure of the paper. Clear and organized.

Special Assignments

Special Assignments

As you make you way through this course you will be asked to do a number of quizzes, assignments, and discussions (if this is an online or hybrid class) specific to the content of the Chapter in question.

In addition to these activities are these "Special Assignments". These are assignments that engage you in applying multiple skills and the knowledge from this course to produce a more substantive product.

Many of these assignments have been developed to address larger and more global learning outcomes within the context of the content of this course. These learning outcomes, however, are usually applicable to nearly every other area of your life as well.

These learning outcomes are largely associated with the AAC&U VALUE Rubric learning outcomes that were presented early in this book. Example of the types of skills you will develop in these assignments include, but are not limited to:

- Critical Thinking
- Creative Thinking
- Information Literacy
- Teamwork
- Writing
- Quantitative Reasoning
- and many more...

The details for these assignments can be found here. Due dates and other resources will be provided by your instructor.

Cultural Dimensions of Childbirth

Purpose

Earth Birth

The basic biology of the beginning of life is universal, but cultural norms, values, and expectations vary around the world. Cultures have developed all sorts of rituals and ceremony associated with childbirth (including our own!)

In this assignment we are going to explore some of these cultural practices.

MOVIE - Cultural Practices around Birth among First Nation in British Columbia

I selected this video to provide some examples because I have family in Prince George, BC. My mother lived there when she was alive and my brother, sister-in-law, and niece all still live there.

Skills and Knowledge

You will demonstrate the following skills and knowledge by completing this assignment:

1. Outline general practices that exemplify cultural competency when dealing with pregnancy and childbirth.

2. Identify the expectations, norms, and practices of childbirth within specific cultural traditions.

3. Create training materials for the staff of a theoretical birthing center.

Task

For this assignment you will assume the role of the Training Coordinator for a birthing center. (You can create a name and a place!) The situation is that two distinct cultural groups have emigrated into your area. Your staff does not have any experience with the prenatal, pregnancy, and birthing practices of these people.

Your task is to design a training that will accomplish the following:

1. Increase the cultural competency of your staff when dealing with any culturally based practice.

2. Identify the specific expectations and practices of the two cultural groups that have moved into your area.

Your **primary source** is going to be the document below. You need to select two of the cultural categories identified in this document for your presentation.

Cultural Birthing Practices and Experiences

Format

Your training must be in the form of a slide show (Power Point or Keynote).

Your slides should cover all the major point of your research, be organized and clear, contain supporting and appropriate graphics, and look professional.

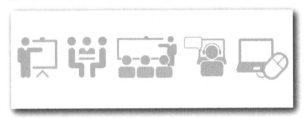

At the beginning it should describe GENERAL PRACTICES of cultural competency (you will need to look this up!)

Then you will move on to presentations on the two cultures.

At the end of the presentation your slide show should also include a list of 5 discussion questions related to

the material. Remember that discussion questions are meant to bring about DISCUSSION, not just a right answer.

Finally, your last slide should include references to all of your sources. Be sure that you cite your sources in APA format.

Formatting a Slide Show

When you are creating each of your individual slides they should be simple and they should NOT contain all of your information…only an outline.

In the "notes" section of each slide I want you to write out what you would say to your audience to support the material that is outlined on the slide.

Criteria for Success

Use the rubric below as a guide to this assignment.

Cultural Competency   20 points

The training clearly outlined generic expectations and practices for professional behavior regarding multicultural practices in pregnancy and childbirth.

Culture #1   20 points

The training covers a comprehensive list of specific cultural practices and any significant meaning behind them.

Culture #2   20 points

The training covers a comprehensive list of specific cultural practices and any significant meaning behind them.

Assessment   20 points

At least 5 discussion questions covering the content of the training.

References   10 points

ALL the information in this assignment should be referenced in APA format on the last slide.

Mechanics   10 points

Spelling, syntax, and organizational structure of materials. Clear and organized. Aesthetic quality to be attractive to audience.

Identity Status

Purpose

"Change is the only constant in life." - Heraclitus

This course is really all about change, and we are constantly changing. Specifically, the ways in which we perceive ourselves and the fate and decisions we make that define us are core to our sense of self.

As adults we are much more in charge of the process of defining ourselves than when we were young. So, we are now a combination of characteristics that have been both bestowed upon us and earned through our choices.

The purpose of this assignment is to highlight the ways in which some aspects of our selves have been ascribed to us through experiences we had no control over, other aspects exist through our specific actions and choices, and that, as adults, we can have several aspects of ourselves in a variety of states of change.

Skills and Knowledge

You will demonstrate the following skills and knowledge by completing this assignment:

1. Identify key areas of early childhood experiences that currently play a role in the definition of self.

2. Apply the Identity Status model to evaluate changes in personal status over time.

Task

The rubric below outlines a list of areas for personal reflection. These include specific incidents associated with the first four stages in Erikson's theory which represent aspects of ourselves that we likely had little control over.

The second area relates to aspects of yourself related to likes, dislikes (hobbies, music, activities, etc.) and vocational/scholastic choices (school, career goals, etc.).

Finally, the third area focuses on areas having to do with the creation of parts of your Relationship Personality. Relationship Personality is an aspect of my Puzzle Pieces theory that we will more fully explore in Young Adulthood, but is built upon experiences leading up to and including adolescence.

To contextualize this into the Puzzle Pieces theory, each of these areas is a single piece (of sorts.) I'm asking you to simply write a paragraph for each one, answering the prompt in the rubric as best you can. The best way to format this assignment would be to start with the title page, and then title each area in bold on its own line, and then write your reflection below the title. This will allow me to easily follow your reflections. Here is an example of one entry:

Industry vs. Inferiority

I went to a very small elementary school in a small, French community in Northern Maine. I was a very active child and had a lot of athletic ability. However, I was the smallest person in the class. I believe that I developed the ability to run very fast due to the need for self-preservation and as a way of compensating for my height. From the start, this became a pattern in my early life that has lasted my entire life. I'm still athletic and feel that my sports (cycling, racquetball, frisbee, soccer, swimming, running, etc.) are very important parts of my identity.

Another interesting aspect of my first couple years in school was the fact that most of my peers were learning English as a second language. The community was a mix of both English and French but many of my friends spoke French at home. The only language at my home, sadly, was English. While I have always wished I had grown up in a dual-language environment, I was also better prepared for the all-English school experience. I remember being called on to read a lot because I could read and speak well in English. This early experience showed me that I was "good at school", another aspect of my identity that stuck with me throughout my life.

Criteria for Success

Use the rubric below as a guide to this assignment.

Title Page   5 points

Standard title page with name, date, course, college name and the name of the assignment.

Trust vs. Mistrust   5 points

As best as you can describe the puzzle piece that is about basic trust in the world. These are largely foreclosed (to a degree) so just describe them.

Autonomy vs. Shame   5 points

As best as you can describe the puzzle piece that is about your degree of autonomy and independence. These are largely foreclosed (to a degree) so just describe them.

Initiative vs. Guilt   5 points

As best as you can describe the puzzle piece that is about your capacity to initiate and plan. These are largely foreclosed (to a degree) so just describe them.

Industry vs. Inferiority   10 points

As best as you can describe the puzzle piece that is about what you are good at and not good at. These are largely foreclosed (to a degree) so just describe them.

Personal Likes and Dislikes   10 points

List two things you like (hobbies, music, etc.) and trace the sequence of changes across different statuses in accordance with Marcia's theory.

Vocational/Job Identity   10 points

Trace the sequence of your journey to discover your current vocational/school identity in accordance with Marcia's theory.

Family Relationship Models   10 points

Describe the piece that was defined by the nature and quality of your first role models for intimate relationships...your parents.

Early Relationships   10 points

Describe the piece that was defined by your first early dating relationships.

Recent and Current Relationships   10 points

Describe your current piece in relation to your recent and current relationships.

Mechanics   10 points

Spelling, syntax, and organizational structure of the paper. Clear and organized.

MOVIE - Identity Status Special Assignment Instructions

Biography Interview

Purpose

Each of us exemplifies a case study of human development. This is particular true of the elderly, who have lived a number of years, survived their trials and challenges, and are now repositories of wisdom that they are willing to share.

Image from www.lifehacker.com

Biography Analysis is a research method utilized in the study of Human Development. By hearing, writing, reading, and analyzing the specific life stories of individuals we gain a unique insight into the diversity, and similarity, of our life stories.

In this class you will be engaging an individual, age 65 or older, in an extended interview...documenting their lives and, just possibly, learning a lot more about your own!

It is my hope that someday I will be able to produce a television show similar to the real "Biography". I want to call it "Maine Biography" and it want to feature just regular people, like the individuals you are going to interview in this class. I wish to show that even those "regular" people often lead very remarkable and interesting lives!

Skills and Knowledge

You will demonstrate the following skills and knowledge by completing this assignment:

1. Demonstrate key interviewing skills, information gathering, and history taking

2. Analyze key concepts in human development from the perspective of a case study

3. Apply these analyses to a process of self-analysis

4. Write a life span biography

Task

Through the entire course you will be required to engage and interview an individual of your choice aged 65 or older. This person can be related to you. In addition to the interview process to write the person's biography you will also be asking them specific questions related to the content of the course.

The point of this aspect of the class is to provide a point of reference for understanding how individuals change over time by conversing with an individual who has undergone many of these changes already. This activity also provides us with a point of reference in discussing the "Historical Clock" or the ways in which being born in a particular time in history impact normal human development.

Step 1 - Finding a Subject

For some of you this may be an easy first step. You may know someone in your family or from work who meets the age criteria and is willing to participate in this study.

For some of you, it may be more of a challenge. We will work together as a class to help you identify potential candidates for this study and to explore communication options. Keep in mind that with today's technology, we do not have to live close to the person!

To communicate to your instructor that you have successfully found a person who is willing to participate in this study, you will need to complete the **Biography Interview Proposal Quiz.**

The content of this quiz is as follows:

2. What is the name of the person you are going to interview for your Biography Interview study.

3. Briefly describe your relationship with this person. How do you know them? If this is a person from your workplace, describe what steps you have taken to get permission to interview this person.

4. I am confident that this person will be able to provide enough information to meet the criteria of this project (T or F)

5. I understand that it is my responsibility to ensure that the life story I get is detailed enough to meet the criteria for this project (T or F)

6. If this person does not meet the age requirement for the project, justify your choice of this person here. If they do you may leave this section blank or pose any specific questions to me here.

You are to take this quiz prior to beginning any aspect of this project. You must score a 100 on this proposal. You are able to take the quiz over and over in order for your plan to be approved.

Part 2 - Planning the Interview

The planning of the interview happens in two ways. First you need to work out a schedule of time with the person (in person, on the phone, video chat, email, etc.) that will be sufficient to get the story.

The other part is to anticipate particular aspects of the person's life that you will want to know about and formulate questions to explore these areas.

While the basic expectation (see below) of the interview is a free flow of story telling, you will want to identify some typical areas of development and particular challenges of development that you will want to explore.

We will be conducting an in-class or Online discussion about these areas and formulating questions that might explore them. To start this process rolling here are some suggestions as to some developmental topics we may wish to explore:

1. Birth information (normal, abnormal, type of birth, early issues).

2. Composition of birth family (parents, siblings, other relatives).

3. Socioeconomic status of early childhood.

4. Typical expectations in the household.

5. First school experiences.

6. Successful or poor teaching/learning experiences.

7. Friends, games, adventures, during childhood.

8. Adolescence

9. Early romantic relationships.

...and I am only scratching the surface here!

Step 3 - Conduct the Interview

If you are really dealing with someone in the later part of their lives they are at the stage in their life where Erikson identified the need to conduct a Life Review. Many elderly people are tying together the threads of their lives and integrating them into a whole.

THEY LIKE TO TALK ABOUT STORIES FROM THE OLD DAYS!

So, since the goal of the **BIOGRAPHY** itself is to get the **STORY**...then you simply ask them to tell you stories.

Since you want to cover the whole lifespan you might end up asking questions like this:

1. What was it like growing up back then?

2. What was school like when you first went there?

3. What was your first job like?

These types of questions get people going on more stories and help fill in the gaps. Your biography itself though, should flow like a single story....it should not read like a question-answer interview.

In addition, there will be times during the class where I'm going to have you ask them about specific aspects of their development...this may lead to more stories and more details about their lives.

Here is a cool video about how to conduct an interview. This is specific for a crisis, but it includes a lot of very helpful tips. (Thank you to Nancy Cronin for finding this resource!)

If you still need some help, there is a page in the Resources chapter at the end of the book with some additional questions or topics to explore.

Step 4 - Organize the Material

This is likely the most complex and demanding aspect of this assignment! Your subject may tell a lot of stories, but they may come out of order! Ultimately you have to submit a story that is a timeline from early life through to their current age. You will need to organize the stories in order across the person's lifespan.

In addition, to enhance this project, you may want to include pictures in your document. If you wanted to get real fancy, you could even insert audio and video into the document (discuss this with your Instructor to explore how to do this.)

Step 5 - Write the Paper

Ultimately you are producing a story of someone's life, not an academic paper. The **Biography Interview Reflection** will take care of the academic part of this process. You are writing a narrative story. It flows like any "biography" that you might read in a book.

Your writing should maintain all of the following:

1. Maintain the "voice" of your writing. If you are going to write in 1st person ("I was born on a

MOVIE - How to Interview People for their Life Story

dark and stormy night in late August...") or 3rd person ("Stan was born on a dark and stormy night in late August...") be sure to maintain this voice in the whole paper.

2. Embrace a story-telling mode of writing that uses language to create pictures in the reader's mind. This is a narrative, not a bullet-point list of events.

3. Details matter. Explore the events themselves but venture to include historical information that is relevant, emotional reactions on the part of the people involved, and current reflections by your subject on these events.

4. If you are going to include media (pictures) these should be contextual (having to do with the story that appears alongside the image) and should include a caption describing the picture, naming the individuals, etc.

Step 6 - Submitting the Paper

The final step is getting the document to your Instructor. A drop box will be provided in Bb, but depending on the size of the file (pictures, audio, and video can take up a lot of space) other options may be available.

If you are submitting a regular written document, the paper should comply with the following expectations:

1. MS Word or PDF format ONLY (no Pages or Google Docs)

2. Double-spaced text, 12 point font, Times New Roman font

3. Title page with the name of the subject, your name, the class and semester/year, etc.

4. Submitted as ONE SINGLE FILE...not multiple files and no attachments. (See your Instructor about this if there is a problem.)

Criteria for Success

Grading someone's life story is impossible. At the end of the day the assignment is a qualitative assignment and its worth is limitless. However, I do feel that if a person is willing to give you the time to participate in this study, you should make best effort to gather a comprehensive story of the individual. We are covering a lot of years. Grading of the Biography Interview will be based simply on the number of pages in the document.

18 Pages or more   100 points

Page count assume the 12 point, Times New Roman font, double-spaced, and does not include extra spaces and/or pictures, title page, etc.

16-17 Pages   90 points

Good effort.

10-15 Pages   80 points

This is minimal and barely acceptable. If you submit a biography with this low page count we will have to have a conversation as to why this happened.

Less than 10 Pages   0 points

Unacceptable work.

Biography Reflection

Purpose

The Biography Interview is a powerful way to conduct research. In this assignment you are going to use a variety of theories and models to analyze stories from you Biography Interview.

This assignment should reflect a high degree of effort on your part to apply what you have learned through this process. **DO NOT APPROACH THIS ASSIGNMENT LIGHTLY!** I'm asking you to get **DEEP.**

You have worked very hard on this project and in this class, it is vital that you make this effort to **REFLECT** on that learning so that you can benefit the most from the process you have gone through.

Skills and Knowledge

You will demonstrate the following skills and knowledge by completing this assignment:

1. Apply a variety of developmental models/theories to an understanding of identified events in a person's life.

2. Apply lessons learned in the Biography assignment to an assessment of one's own life path.

Task

Remember, format your paper so that each of the sections is highlighted by a bold title...this makes it easy for you instructor to locate each part.

Please follow the following outline for the structure of your paper:

Title Page

1. Include your name

2. Assignment name: "Reflection on the Biography of ....(insert your subject's name here)"

3. Name of the course

4. Date

Application of Theory

In this section you will outline three (3) stories from the biography and analyze these stories in light of three DIFFERENT theories or models you have learned about in this class. For each one you will include the following:

1. In bold font, the titles "Theory Application 1", then "Theory Application 2", then "Theory Application 3"

2. At least one paragraph describing the event(s) from the life story that you are going to analyze. This is NOT the analysis itself, this is the story right from your biography told in a way that ensures that the reader understands the story and will be able to connect it to your analysis.

3. A name and description of the theory or model you are going to use to analyze the story.

4. A 1-paragraph analysis of the story where you demonstrate how the theory is applied, or supported (example), or contested (non-example, when the person did not follow the predictions in the theory).

There are many theories and models from the course that you can choose from. As you make your way through the material, be sure to ask your instructor of the current topic is a model or not.

Some examples of these may include the following:

- Prenatal Development
- Critical Periods
- Physical and Motor Development
- Theory of Mind
- Self-Perception
- Piaget's Genetic Epistemology
- Information Processing
- Cultural Identity
- Language Development
- Erikson's Psychosocial Development Theory
- Attachment
- Gender Role Development
- Looking Glass Self
- Vygotsky's Theory
- Intelligence (including exceptionality)

- Multiple Intelligence Theory
- Family Systems Theory
- Parenting Styles
- Social Groups (Friends, Work, Family)
- Perspective Taking
- Puberty
- Elkind's Adolescent Egocentrism
- Moral Development (Kohlberg and/or Gilligan)
- Identify Development
- Rites of Passage
- Possible Selves
- Puzzle Pieces
- Love and Intimacy
- Sternberg's Triangular Theory of Love
- Reflective Judgement

- Holland's Occupational Theory
- Work and Family
- Midlife Crisis (Marcia's Theory)
- Middle Age Family Changes (included Empty Next Syndrome)
- Aging
- Continuity Theory
- Late Life Cognitive Development
- Mental Health and Aging
- Wisdom
- Grieving
- Chronic Illness
- Disability

Please note: Concepts such as "The Developmental Perspective", "Developmental Clocks", "Nature vs. Nurture", "Continuity vs. Discontinuity", and "Universal vs. Contextual" CANNOT be used...these are not THEORIES or MODELS.

Historical Perspective

Select an event in your subject's life that relates to local, regional, national, or world events that were going on at the time. Conduct some additional outside research on that event. Describe the event and interrelate your subject's perspective on these events.

Learning Wisdom

It is hard to write a Biography of a person without being personally moved by it. Reflect on some perspectives you may have had about the "world" or "education" or just about any topic. How has getting to know the historical perspective of this person changed, in any way, your perspective on these subjects.

Interviewing Skills

This activity required that you interview someone about intimate details in their lives. Reflect on what you have learned about communicating with others, asking questions, and listening to stories.

What will happen to this story?

Explain what is going to happen with the Biography you put together? Did your subject get a copy? Do other family members want copies? Will you publish it? Reflect on who might be interested in reading this story. Consider doing any number of these things with the story because you have gathered a very important part of history.

Criteria for Success

Use the rubric below as a guide to this assignment.

Title Page   5 points
Standard title page with name, date, course, college name and the name of the assignment.

Application 1   15 points
All components - title of theory/concept, definition, story, analysis - Story aligns with theory/concept, analysis displays an understanding of the theory/concept.

Application 2   15 points

All components - title of theory/concept, definition, story, analysis - Story aligns with theory/concept, analysis displays an understanding of the theory/concept.

Application 3   15 points

All components - title of theory/concept, definition, story, analysis - Story aligns with theory/concept, analysis displays an understanding of the theory/concept.

Historical Perspective   10 points

Detailed description of historical event and subject's perspective.

Learning Wisdom   10 points

Reflection on personal perspective prior to the project and how it has been changed.

Interviewing Skills   10 points

Reflection on communication skills, question skills, and listening.

What will happen to this story? 10 points

Explain what has or will happen to the story. Explain who might be interested in the story.

Mechanics   10 points

Spelling, syntax, and organizational structure of the paper. Clear and organized.

Appendix

Microsoft 365

www.office.com

Microsoft 365

All students at KVCC are provided with free access to Microsoft Office! We have a deal with them that allow currently registered students to download all the Office apps to their computer and to any mobile device (there are versions of Word, Excel, and PowerPoint that will work on our tablet and/or phone.)

This tool will also give you access to other Microsoft apps such as Teams (KVCC uses this to hold virtual meetings), OneDrive (online file storage), OneNote (organize information), and Outlook (email client).

To access these tools you need to visit the link below and use your KVCC user name and password to register.

Monitor on Psychology

Monitor on Psychology

The world of psychology is ever-changing and it is difficult to keep up with all of it. The American Psychological Association publishes a magazine called Monitor on Psychology.

Monitor is a magazine geared toward general readership that explores emerging topics of importance to psychology. It presents articles and research in a very readable, typical magazine format.

Access to the Monitor is free through their website or the app!

Monitor on Psychology Website

Dr. K's Psychobabble

Dr. K's YouTube Channel

Having had to make small recordings explaining psychological concepts for my online students, I decided to turn those efforts into my own YouTube channel!

You may find some of these videos embedded within this CourseBook.

Visit Dr. K's Psychobabble YouTube Channel

Made in the USA
Coppell, TX
13 September 2023